Seafood
COOKBOOK

by Carol Ann Shipman

hancock

house

ISBN 0-88839-514-0
ISBN 0-88839-584-1 (Alaskan edition)
Copyright © 2004 Carol Ann Shipman

Cataloging in Publication Data

Shipman, Carol Ann, 1944–
   Seafood cookbook / Carol Ann Shipman.

   (Nature's gourmet series)
   Includes index.
   ISBN 0-88839-514-0 — ISBN 0-88839-584-1 (Alaskan ed.)

   1. Cookery (Seafood) I. Title. II. Series.
TX747.S54 2004   641.6'92   C2003-910987-9

Printed in China—JADE

Editing: Nancy Miller
Series design and production: Nando DeGirolamo
Photographic sources listed on page 93.

Published simultaneously in Canada and the United States by

HANCOCK HOUSE PUBLISHERS LTD.
19313 Zero Avenue, Surrey, B.C. V3S 9R9
(604) 538-1114 Fax (604) 538-2262

HANCOCK HOUSE PUBLISHERS
1431 Harrison Avenue, Blaine, WA 98230-5005
(604) 538-1114 Fax (604) 538-2262
Web Site: www.hancockhouse.com *email:* sales@hancockhouse.com

dedication

This book is dedicated to my son Mark Kenneth Loeppky, with love.

acknowledgments

I was very fortunate to work with a wonderful team to produce this book. I appreciate and thank all the people who were involved. I give special thanks to Richard Shipman, my husband, and also my son John and his beautiful wife, Susan, for the constant support and understanding testing endless recipes for all of my cookbooks.

To my publisher David Hancock, who shared my vision for the series, thank you for your patience and enthusiasm for this book.

Thanks again to Nando DeGirolamo, for his outstanding design for the entire series.

I'm very fortunate to have wonderful friends, such as our long time friend, Tom Gallaugher, who has eaten and, I think, enjoyed so many of the dishes in this book— a man that when he laughs, it warms the soul.

A special thank you goes to my twin sister Lorna May Matthew, for her ongoing support and the many late night calls to see how the books were coming.

Thank you!

contents

appetizers

What is life without an oyster? An empty shell. Oysters are like no other food. They impart a feeling of well-being and happiness, cure digestive problems, prod jaded appetites and persuade men of powers they didn't know they had.

Rabbit Hill Inn Shrimp and Corn Pancake

YIELD 15 pancakes

1-1/4 cups	**flour**	310 mL
1 tbsp	**baking powder**	15 mL
5	**eggs**	5
1-1/2 cups	**milk**	375 mL
6 tbsp	**melted butter**	90 mL
1 tsp	**salt**	5 mL
1 cup	**baby shrimp** cooked	250 mL
1-1/2 cups	**fresh corn**	375 mL

In a bowl, make a well with the flour and baking powder. Add eggs in the center and mix well. Slowly add milk and butter. Strain to remove lumps. Add salt, corn and shrimp. Melt butter in a 5-inch nonstick sauté pan. Cook corn cakes as you do pancakes, cook on each side until golden brown.

The Inn on the Common Smoked Seafood Mousse

SERVES 8 – 10

1 envelope	**unflavored gelatin**	15 mL
1/4 cup	**cold water**	250 mL
1/2 cup	**boiling water**	125 mL
1/3 cup	**mayonnaise** or **plain yogurt**	75 mL
3 tbsp	**fresh dill** chopped	45 mL
1 tbsp	**grated onion**	15 mL
1/2 tbsp	**lemon juice**	7.5 mL
1/4 tbsp	**lime juice**	7.5 mL
1/4 tsp	**cayenne pepper**	1 mL
1/4 tsp	**paprika**	1 mL
salt and pepper, to taste		
1 cup	**smoked trout** flaked	250 mL
1 cup	**smoked shrimp** finely chopped	250 mL
1 cup	**whipping cream**	250 mL

In a large bowl, soften the gelatin in the cold water. Stir in boiling water and keep stirring until the gelatin is dissolved. Add the mayonnaise (or yogurt), dill, onion, lemon and lime juices, cayenne pepper, paprika, salt and pepper; whisk until blended. Divide this mixture into two separate bowls. Fold the smoked trout into one bowl; fold the smoked shrimp into the other. Whip the cream to soft peaks and fold half into each bowl. Layer the 2 mousses in separate molds or one large clear glass bowl. Chill overnight, covered. Unmold and garnish with dill. Serve with marinated tomato salad and crackers.

hrimp and
rosciutto Kebabs

ak bamboo skewers, if using, in a large bowl
f cold water for at least 30 minutes before
sing. In a large bowl, combine the olive oil,
arlic, salt and pepper. Add the shrimp and
ushrooms and stir to thoroughly coat. Set
side for 15 minutes. Cut the prosciutto into
to 5 inch strips. Preheat the grill.

ake one shrimp from the marinade and top
ith a sage leaf. Wrap the shrimp in a piece
f prosciutto and thread on skewer. Add one
f the marinated mushrooms, followed by
nother prosciutto-wrapped shrimp. Continue
ith the remaining ingredients.

et the shrimp skewers on the heated grill
nd cook until the shrimp are pink and the
ushrooms lightly browned, 2 to 3 minutes.
urn the skewers and continue grilling until
he shrimp is just opaque through (cut one
test), about 2 minutes longer. Arrange the
kewers on a platter for serving.

SERVES 4

1/3 cup	**olive oil**	75 mL
2	**cloves of garlic** minced	2
salt and freshly ground pepper		
1 lb	**large shrimp** peeled and deveined	454 g
6 tbsp	**small mushrooms**	90 mL
4 tbsp	**prosciutto** thinly sliced	60 mL
8-12	**sage leaves** halved, if large	8-12

*hrimp and
roscuitto Kebabs*

Smoked Black Cod Cakes

SERVES 4

1-1/2 lbs	**smoked black cod**	681 g
1/2	**red bell pepper** cored, seeded and finely diced	1/2
1	**stalk celery** finely diced	1
3	**eggs**	3
1-1/2 tbsp	**Dijon-style mustard**	22.5 mL
1 tbsp	**minced or pressed garlic**	15 mL
3 tbsp	**parsley** finely chopped	45 mL
4	**dashes Tabasco sauce**	4
5 cups	**soft white bread crumbs**	1250 mL
	oil for frying	

PIQUANT PEPPER RELISH

2	**red bell pepper** roasted and peeled	2
2	**yellow bell peppers** roasted and peeled	2
2	**medium tomatoes** cored and peeled	2
3 tbsp	**brown sugar**	45 mL
3 tbsp	**vinegar**	45 mL
1/4 tsp	**ground allspice**	1 mL
1/4 tsp	**dried red pepper flakes**	1 mL
	salt and freshly ground pepper to taste	

To prepare the relish, slice the roasted peppers and tomatoes into thin strips and mix together. In a small saucepan, combine the sugar, vinegar, allspice, red pepper flakes, with salt and pepper to taste and heat gently until the sugar is dissolved. Pour the hot liquid over the roasted peppe mixture. Set aside.

Remove the skin and bones from the smoke black cod and flake it into a medium bowl. Add the bell pepper, celery, eggs, mustard, garlic and half of the parsley. Season with Tabasco, salt and pepper. Stir in 1-1/2 cups (375 mL) of the breadcrumbs until the mixture is thoroughly combined.

Shape the cod cakes into 1/4-cup balls and place in a container covered with the remaining breadcrumbs and parsley. Sprinkle some of the breadcrumbs over the cakes and chill for 30 minutes. This helps make the cakes easier to handle, and the crumbs make a nice crust.

Heat about 1-inch of oil in a skillet over medium heat. Discard excess breadcrumbs from the cod cakes and fry until evenly golden brown, about 3 minutes on each side. Serve the cakes hot with the piquant pepper relish.

Smoked Black Cod Cakes

Maude's Courtyard Bed & Breakfast Scampi Lorenzo

ound out chicken breasts and cut into rips to make chicken tenders. Peel and evein uncooked shrimp. Wrap individual hicken strips around shrimp and hold with oothpicks. Marinate shrimp wrapped in hicken in Italian salad dressing overnight. auté butter, finely chopped garlic and mon juice. Add shrimp/chicken and sear n high heat, constantly turning the shrimp. ransfer to grill and finish cooking. Arrange n a bed of lettuce and fresh cut lemon, prinkle with fresh parsley.

SERVES 4

4	large boneless, skinless chicken breasts	4
12	medium to large shrimp	12
	Italian salad dressing	
	butter	
	lemon juice	
3	fresh garlic cloves	3
	fresh parsley	
	capers optional	

Chef Carol's Hot Mushroom Turnovers

lend cream cheese and 1/2 cup (125 mL) utter; add flour to form soft dough. Wrap ough in waxed paper. Refrigerate at least hour. Sauté mushrooms and onion in 3 ablespoons (45 mL) butter, until tender. dd salt, thyme and 2 tablespoons (30 mL) our. Remove from heat. Stir in sour cream. oll out dough and cut 3-inch circles. Place teaspoon (5 mL) of mushroom mixture on ach circle. Brush edges of pastry with egg. old pastry over filling to form turnover. inch edges together with fork; prick top ith fork to let steam escape. Place on ngreased cookie sheets. Repeat procedure ith remaining dough and mushroom lling. Brush turnovers with egg. Bake at 50°F (230°C) for 12 to 15 minutes or until olden brown. These turnovers are great ith seafood.

YIELD 12 –18

1 cup	cream cheese	250 mL
1/2 cup	butter softened	125 mL
1-1/2 cups	flour sifted	375 mL
3 tbsp	butter	45 mL
3	10-ounce (320-mL) cans mushroom stems and pieces, drained and chopped	900 mL
1/2	large onion minced	1/2
1 tsp	salt	5 mL
1/4 tsp	thyme	1 mL
2 tbsp	flour	30 mL
1/4 cup	sour cream	60 mL
1	egg beaten	1

Gingered Fruit Salsa

In a medium bowl, stir together the wine, cranberries, vinegar and fresh and crystallized ginger. Let sit for 15 minutes, then add the papaya, pear and strawberries. Toss to mix well and serve.

SERVES 8

1/4 cup	**dry white wine**	60 mL
1/4 cup	**dried cranberries** optional	60 mL
2 tbsp	**seasoned rice vinegar or white wine vinegar**	30 mL
1 tbsp	**ginger** fresh, minced	15 mL
1 tbsp	**ginger** minced, crystallized	15 mL
1	**papaya** peeled, seeded and diced	1
1	**pear** halved, cored and diced	1
3/4 cup	**strawberries** stemmed and sliced	175 mL

Gingered Fruit Salsa

Soy Glazed Mushrooms with Smoked Five Spice Shrimp

oy Glazed Mushrooms vith Smoked Five Spice hrimp

lake the sauce by blending the water, soy auce, sugar and cornstarch. Set aside. Heat wok or large skillet over medium-high eat. Add the oil and swirl the pan to coat he sides. Add the garlic and ginger and auté until aromatic, about 15 seconds. Sear he mushrooms in the hot oil until nicely rowned and tender, about 4 minutes. Add he sherry, shrimp and water chestnuts. Stir he sauce to thoroughly mixed and pour it ito the wok. Cook, stirring constantly, until he sauce thickens and the ingredients are venly coated, 2 minutes more. Transfer the hrimp mixture to a warmed serving dish, orinkle with the green onion and serve nmediately.

SERVES 2

1/3 cup	**water**	75 mL
3 tbsp	**soy sauce** preferably reduced-sodium	45 mL
2 tbsp	**sugar**	30 mL
1-1/2 tsp	**cornstarch**	7.5 mL
2 tbsp	**peanut or vegetable oil**	30 mL
2	**cloves garlic** minced or pressed	2
1 tsp	**minced or grated ginger**	5 mL
4 cups	**mushrooms** quartered use an assortment, such as buttons, shiitakes, oyster mushrooms	1000 mL
2 tsp	**medium-dry sherry, chicken stock or wine**	10 mL
1 lb	**smoked five-spice shrimp** or other smoked shrimp	454 g
1/2 cup	**sliced water chestnuts**	125 mL
1	**green onion** thinly sliced	1

Spanish Style Mussels with Olives

SERVES 4

2 tsp	**olive oil**	10 mL
1 cup	**onion** chopped	250 mL
4	**cloves garlic** chopped	4
pinch dried red pepper flakes		
3 lbs	**mussels** scrubbed and debearded	1362 g
1/4 cup	**medium-dry** **or dry sherry**	60 mL
1 cup	**diced tomato**	250 mL
1/2 cup	**green olives** chopped	125 mL
1	**juice of 1 lemon**	1
2 tbsp	**parsley** chopped	30 mL

Heat the oil in a large skillet over medium-high heat. Add the onion and garlic and cook until aromatic and slightly tender, stirring often, 2 to 3 minutes. Stir in the red pepper flakes, then add the mussels, stirring so the are evenly coated in the vegetable mixture. Add the sherry, cover the pan and steam until the mussels just begin to open, 4 to 5 minutes. Add the tomato, olives, lemon juic and parsley and gently stir just to mix. Spoon the mussels onto small individual plates, drizzle the cooking liquids over the serve.

Spanish Style Mussel
with Olive

an Antonio Seafood Cocktail

ombine salsa and ketchup, season with a queeze of fresh lemon juice; transfer to a rving bowl and chill. To serve, place the owl on a leaf lettuce-lined platter and rround with cooked and chilled shrimp, allops or crabmeat or a combination of three.

SERVES 4

1 cup	**Pace Picante Sauce**	250 mL
	or Pace Thick & Chunky Salsa	
1 cup	**ketchup**	250 mL
1	**squeeze of fresh lemon juice**	1
	shrimp, scallops, crabmeat	

eafood Dip

a small bowl, cream together the cream eese, sour cream, and mayonnaise until ry smooth then add lemon juice, parsley, een onions and Worcestershire sauce. nce mixture is well incorporated, set ixture aside.

uté Mixture

skillet on medium heat, sauté the gredients until lightly golden. Once sautéed, t aside to cool. When cooled down, mix uté mixture into seafood dip. Mix well.

dd salt, pepper, and grated cheese. Slowly ix the seafood into mixture. Place in eased baking dishes. Fill baking dishes 3/4 ll and bake in a 350°F (175°C) degree oven til lightly golden and bubbling hot. Remove om oven and let sit for a few minutes before rving. Garnish with a sprinkle of grated eese and chopped parsley on top of each rving dish. Serve with either slices of asted bagette, chunks of sourdough bread, ustinis or crackers. This dip freezes onderfully. You can prepare it ahead of ne and take it from the freezer, to the en, and to the table. Enjoy!

SERVES 4 – 6

2 cups	**cream cheese**	500 ml
1 cup	**sour cream**	250 ml
1 cup	**mayonnaise**	250 ml
1 tbsp	**lemon juice**	15 ml
2 tbsp	**chopped parsley**	30 ml
1/2 cup	**green onions** chopped	125 ml
1 tsp	**Lea & Perrins Worcestershire sauce**	5 ml

SAUTÉ MIXTURE

2 tbsp	**butter**	30 ml
1/2-3/4 cups	**green pepper** finely chopped	125-175 ml
1/2 cup	**mushrooms** finely chopped	125 ml
1 tbsp	**garlic** finely chopped	15 ml
3/4 cup	**Asiago cheese** grated	175 ml
	salt and pepper to taste	
1-1/2 cups	**seafood** cooked	375 ml
	assorted shrimp, scallops and crab	

Braised Scallops with Grapefruit and Walnuts

SERVES 4

2	**pink grapefruit**	2
1 lb	**sea scallops**	454 g
1/2 cup	**flour seasoned with salt and pepper**	125 mL
2 tbsp	**walnut oil or olive oil**	30 mL
1/2 cup	**walnuts** finely chopped	125 mL
2 tbsp	**chives or green onion** minced, for garnish	30 mL

Cut both ends from one of the grapefruits ju to the flesh. Set it upright on the chopping board and use the knife to cut away the pe and skin, following the curve of the fruit. Holding the peeled grapefruit in your hand slide the knife blade down one side of a section, cutting it from the membrane. Cu down the other side of the section and remove it. (Work over a bowl to catch the sections and juice.) Continue for the remai ing sections, turning back flaps of membran like the pages of a book. Squeeze the juic from the second grapefruit and combine with any juice from the first. Alternatively you can seed and section a hand-peeled grap fruit, but the membranes will be tough and the pith bitter.

Lightly coat the scallops in seasoned flour, patting to remove the excess. Heat the oil i a medium skillet, preferably non-stick. Wh the oil is very hot, add the scallops and coc over medium heat until browned, about 1 minute per side. Transfer the scallops to a plate and set aside.

Add the grapefruit juice to the skillet and bring to a boil. Stir in the walnuts, then ad the scallops and grapefruit sections to the pan and simmer gently until the scallops a cooked to taste, 2 to 3 minutes. Arrange th scallops, grapefruit and sauce on individu plates, sprinkle with chives and serve.

*raised Scallops with
rapefruit and Walnuts*

Crab Dip

ince crabmeat, grate eggs very fine and
ince onion, mayonnaise, add mayonnaise
d chili sauce. Mix together, season with
lt and pepper. Chill.

YIELD 2 3/4 cups

1 cup	**crab meat**	250 mL
1 cup	**mayonnaise**	250 mL
1/2 cup	**chili sauce**	125 mL
2	**hard-boiled eggs** grated	2
1	**green onion** minced	1
	salt and pepper, to taste	

Chef Carol's Crab Louie

ince the imitation crabmeat; add remainder
the ingredients. Mix well. Chill for 1 hour
fore serving. This will hold in the
frigerator for one week.

rve with Ritz Original Crackers, the only
acker that complements this appetizer.

SERVES 6 – 8

1 lb	**imitation crabmeat** minced	454 g
2 tsp	**chili sauce**	10 mL
2 tsp	**green onion** chopped	10 mL
1 tsp	**vinegar**	5 mL
1 tsp	**horseradish**	5 mL
1 tsp	**yellow mustard**	5 mL
1/2 tsp	**sugar**	2 mL
1/4 tsp	**paprika**	1 mL
	salt and pepper	
1/2 cup	**mayonnaise**	125 mL
1/2 cup	**sour cream**	125 mL

soup & salad

Shrimp or prawn, that is the question. When is a shrimp a prawn?
Is scampi a species or a dish? Confused? You're not alone. Our advice?
A shrimp is a shrimp. Anything else is simply marketing.

SERVES 6 – 8

FISH STOCK

2 lbs	**fish bones and trimmings**	900 g
4 cups	**water** or more if desired	1000 mL
2 tbsp	**leek** white part, roughly chopped	30 mL
2 tbsp	**carrot** chopped	30 mL
2 tbsp	**celery** chopped	30 mL
2 tbsp	**mushrooms trimmings**	30 mL
1/4 cup	**dry white wine**	60 mL
1	**egg white and crushed eggshell**	1

SOUP

	fish stock	
1/2 cup	**salmon** cut in diamond shape	125 mL
1/2 cup	**brill** cut in diamond shape	125 mL
2 tbsp	**leek** green part, cut in fine strips	30 mL
2 tbsp	**celery** cut in fine strips	30 mL
1	**carrot** minced	1
	sprigs of dill	
	pink peppercorns	

Salmon Soup

Stock

Reduce wine to half in large saucepan. Add vegetables, fish bones, trimmings and water. Simmer gently for 20 minutes. Season and simmer for a further 5 minutes. Skim occasionally. Strain through muslin, reserving 1 tablespoon (15 mL) of solids.

Clarify

Return stock to a clean pan. Add reserved solids, egg white and shell. Bring to a boil gently, whisking continuously. Carefully strain through double thickness of muslin.

Complete the Soup

Add prepared leek, carrot and celery to clarified stock. Cook for three minutes. Add salmon and brill. Simmer for 2 minutes. Scatter pink peppercorns and sprigs of dill over soup before serving in warmed soup bowls.

SERVES 4

1-1/4 cups	**crabmeat**	300 mL
1 lb	**fresh spinach** chopped	454 g
1	**onion** chopped	1
2	**potatoes** large cubes	2
2 tbsp	**butter**	30 mL
2 cups	**seafood stock** see sauces and stock for recipes	500 mL
2 cups	**milk**	500 mL
1/4 cup	**cream**	60 mL
	salt and pepper, to taste	
	pinch of nutmeg	

Crab and Spinach Soup

Sauté vegetables in melted butter; season. Add stock and milk; simmer until vegetables soften. Liquidize soup in blender or food processor and return to saucepan. Add crabmeat, cream and nutmeg. Heat through before serving with a swirl of cream.

Tropical Mahimahi Salad in a Pita

Preheat the broiler. In a small bowl, mix the honey mustard, vinegar, yogurt, ginger and salt until smooth. Put the mahimahi skin side down on broiler rack and spread 2 (30 mL) tablespoons of the mustard mixture on top. Reserve the rest for dressing the salad. Broil the mahimahi 4 to 5 inches from the heat until the fish is just opaque through, 6 to 10 minutes, depending on the thickness. Remove from oven and let stand while preparing the salad.

Halve the small cucumbers lengthwise and slice crosswise 1/8 inch thick. In a large bowl, toss the cucumbers, mangoes, radishes and cilantro. Peel the skin from the mahimahi and break the flesh into chunks. Add the mahimahi to the salad mixture, pour the reserved dressing on top and gently mix. Taste and adjust seasonings. Half-fill each pita bread with sprouts and spoon in the mahimahi salad on top.

SERVES 4

6 tbsp	**honey mustard**	90 mL
2 tbsp	**cider vinegar**	30 mL
2 tbsp	**plain yogurt**	30 mL
1/2 tsp	**kosher salt**	2 mL
1 lb	**mahimahi fillet** skin on, 3/4-inch thick	454 g
1/3 lb	**pickling-size cumbers** skin on, washed and dried	340.5 g
2 cups	**mangoes** in 1/2-inch dice	500 mL
2 cups	**radishes** very thinly sliced	500 mL
1 cup	**cilantro or parsley** minced	250 mL
4	**large pita breads** halved and warmed	4
2 cups	**onion or spicy sprouts**	500 mL

Tropical Mahimahi Salad in a Pita

Lobster and Fennel Salad with Carrot Ginger Sauce

SERVES 4

2	**fennel bulbs**	2
	trimmed and very thinly sliced	
1/2	**red onion**	1/2
	thinly sliced	
1	**orange**	1
	peeled and sectioned	
4	**lobsters**	4
	cooked and shelled, about 1-1/4 pounds each	
1 tbsp	**grated ginger**	15 mL

LEMON OIL

1/2 cup	**virgin olive oil**	125 mL
3 tbsp	**freshly squeezed lemon juice**	45 mL
1/4 tsp	salt	1/4 tsp

CARROT GINGER SAUCE

8 tbsp	**ginger**	120 mL
	grated	
2 cups	**carrot juice**	500 mL
	stirring with 4 (20 mL) arrowroot or cornstarch	
1/4 cup	**rice vinegar**	60 mL
1/4 tsp	**cayenne pepper**	1 mL
3 tbsp	**lime juice**	45 mL
	salt, to taste	

Carrot Sauce

For the carrot sauce; grate the ginger and squeeze to extract the juice (you should have 2 to 3 tablespoons juice). Discard the pulp and set aside the juice.

Lemon Oil

To make the lemon oil, combine all the ingredients in a small bowl and stir to mix well. Set aside.

Put the 2 cups (500 mL) carrot juice in a small pan and bring to a boil. Stir the carrot juice-cornstarch mixture and whisk it into the boiling carrot juice. Reduce the heat and simmer for 1 minute. Take the pan from the heat, add the ginger juice, vinegar and cayenne and set aside to cool. When cool, stir in the lime juice and season to taste with salt.

In a large bowl, combine the fennel, red onion and orange. Sprinkle lemon oil over to taste and toss gently to coat. Set aside.

Cut the lobster tail pieces into slices (medallions) and put them in another large bowl with the rest of the lobster, ginger, lemon oil and salt to taste. Toss to coat. Arrange the fennel salad in the center of large individual plates. Top the salad with the lobster pieces and drizzle the sauce around. Serve immediately.

Lobster and Fennel Salad with Carrot Ginger Sauce

Kalani Oceanside Retreat, Chef Alaina Lynch's Hawaiian Seafood Soup

SERVES 4 – 6

2 tbsp	**olive oil**	30 mL
2	**medium onions** coarsely diced	2
2 tbsp	**ginger** minced	30 mL
3	**garlic cloves** minced	3
2	**jalapeños** seeded, minced	2
2 cups	**canned plum tomatoes**	500 mL
2 tbsp	**fresh lemon juice**	30 mL
1-1/2 tbsp	**paprika**	23 mL
2/3 cup	**coconut milk**	150 mL
1/2 cup	**macadamia nuts** finely ground	125 mL
1/2 cup	**loosely packed cilantro leaves** leaving a few whole leaves for garnish	125 mL
2 cups	**chicken stock**	500 mL
1/2 lb	**peeled shrimp** fresh	227 g
1/2 lb	**medium scallops**	227 g
1/2 lb	**firm fish fillet** tuna, snapper, swordfish cut in 1/2-inch cubes	227 g
1 tsp	**pepper**	5 mL
	salt to taste	

Heat oil in large pan, add onions and cook over low heat for 15 minutes. Peel and mince garlic and ginger. Stem, seed and mince jalapeños. Coarsely chop tomatoes and reserve juice. Stir into pan the ginger, garlic, jalapeños, half of the tomatoes, all the reserved tomato juice, lemon juice and paprika. Cook for 2 minutes and then add coconut milk. Put macadamia nuts in food processor, process until finely ground, add to soup. Put cilantro leaves in processor and chop; add half the leaves to soup. Transfer soup to processor and puree, adding stock with machine still running. Return to pan, add remaining tomatoes and chopped cilantro. Bring soup to a boil. Season with salt and black pepper. Cover and keep warm (can be cooked, covered and refrigerated up to 2 days.) If soup has been refrigerated, bring to simmer just before serving. While soup is still very hot add shrimp, scallops and fish. Keep lid on for 5 minutes to allow hot liquid to cook fish. Be careful not to overcook. Serve immediately and garnish with cilantro leaves.

Dockside Guest Quarters New England Clam Chowder

Drain and chop clams, reserving liquid (may substitute #5 can chopped clams). Fry salt pork in a heavy pan until all fat is rendered; add onions and celery and brown lightly. Add butter; melt. Blend in flour and stir constantly for 5 minutes. Add clams, milk, potatoes, clam liquid, bay leaf and thyme. Cook until the potatoes are tender. If desired, add fish and or shellfish to make seafood chowder.

SERVES 4

4 cups	**shucked clams**	1000 mL
1/3 lb	**salt pork**	150 g
1	**large onion** minced	1
2	**ribs celery** minced	2
2	**large potatoes** diced	2
1	**bay leaf**	1
1/2 tsp	**thyme**	2 mL
4 cups	**milk** scalded (may use half & half cream for thicker soup)	1000 mL
1/2 cup	**butter**	125 mL
1/4 cup	**flour**	60 mL
	salt and pepper	

Rock Eddy Bluff Farm Salmon Chowder

Sauté onion, celery and pepper in oil until onion is transparent. Add potatoes and water and cook until potatoes are tender. Flake salmon with a fork as it is added to the pot along with milk and cream. Let simmer (do not boil) for 1 hour; add butter. Sprinkle with paprika for added color.

SERVES 2 – 3

1	**small onion** finely chopped	1
1/2 cup	**celery** diced	125 mL
1/4 cup	**green pepper** diced	60 mL
	cooking oil	
3	**small potatoes** chopped	3
1 cup	**water**	250 mL
1	**213 g can salmon** do not drain	1
1 cup	**milk**	250 mL
1 cup	**cream**	250 mL
2 tbsp	**butter**	30 mL
	paprika	

Seafood Pozole

SERVES 6

1	**small onion** thinly sliced	1
2 cups	**yellow hominy** drained and rinsed	500 mL
3/4 lb	**rockfish fillet**	340 g
1	**lime** cut in 6 wedges	1
2 tsp	**olive oil or salad oil**	10 mL
3 cups	**low-salt** **chicken broth**	750 mL
2 cups	**diced tomatoes**	500 mL
1/2 cup	**green chilies** chopped	125 mL
2 tsp	**ground cumin**	10 mL
	salsa or hot pepper sauce optional	
	seafood alternatives snapper, cod, orange roughy, shrimp	

Rinse the fish, pat dry and cut into 3/4-inch cubes (discard any bones you discover while cutting the fish). Heat the oil in a large skillet over medium-high heat, add the onion and cook, stirring often, until the onion is tender, about 5 minutes. Add the hominy, chicken broth, tomatoes and their juice, chilies and cumin. Cover the pan and bring to a boil; reduce the heat and simmer 5 minutes.

Add the fish; simmer and stir gently until the fish flakes when prodded with a fork, 2 to 4 minutes. Ladle the soup into bowls. Squeeze the juice of 1 lime wedge into each bowl of soup. Serve salsa or hot pepper sauce alongside to season to taste.

Seafood Pozole

The Nautilus House of Cape Cod Outrageous Seafood Bisque

Bring chicken stock to a boil. Add potatoes, onions, bay leaf, thyme, garlic, salt and pepper. Simmer until vegetables are barely tender, about 15 minutes. Add half of all seafood and cook for about 5 minutes until seafood is cooked through. Remove bay leaf.

Place mixture, a little at a time, in blender and puree. Place pureed soup mixture into soup kettle. Add remaining seafood and cook until seafood is done. Stir in egg yolks, which have been blended with whipping cream. Cook for 2 minutes while stirring, turn heat off. Add white wine according to taste. Return to heat for several minutes. Serve either hot or cold with paprika or nutmeg garnish.

SERVES 6 – 8

4 cups	**chicken broth**	1000 mL
6	**medium potatoes** peeled, diced	6
2	**medium onions** coarsely chopped	2
1	**bay leaf**	1
1/2 tsp	**thyme**	2 mL
1/4 tsp	**garlic** minced	1 mL
1 tsp	**salt**	5 mL
	dash of fresh pepper	
1 cup	**scallops** chopped	250 mL
1 cup	**shrimp** chopped	250 mL
1 cup	**lobster** chopped	250 mL
1 cup	**crab meat** chopped	250 mL
2	**egg yolks**	2
1/2-1 cup	**whipping cream** depending on how thick you like bisque	125-250 mL
	paprika or nutmeg for garnish	
1/2 cup	**white wine**	125 mL

Ippolito's Seafood Gumbo

Cube all fish and place in refrigerator. Peel and clean shrimp (tails should come off). Chop all vegetables (not too fine). Melt butter in pan. When it starts to foam, add vegetables and chicken broth. Cook to soft on a low flame. In large pot, boil two cups (500 mL) of water. When boiling, add tomato paste and cubed fish. Let simmer on medium heat for 30 minutes. Add pan mixture to other ingredients in pot and season with cayenne, salt and pepper. Stir to thicken.

SERVES 8 – 10

3-1/2 lbs	**white fish** (sea bass, halibut, monkfish, snapper)	1.5 kg
1 lb	**fresh or pasteurized lump crabmeat**	454 g
1-1/2 lbs	**large fresh shrimp**	700 g
1-1/2 lbs	**fresh okra**	700 g
4	**red peppers**	4
4	**green peppers**	4
1	**onion**	1
1 lb	**mushrooms**	454 g
4 cups	**tomato paste**	1000 mL
4 cups	**chicken broth**	1000 mL
2 cups	**butter**	500 mL
2 cups	**water**	500 mL
	cayenne pepper, to taste	
	salt and ground pepper, to taste	

Claudia's Seafood Chowder

SERVES 8 – 10

1 tbsp	**butter**	15 mL
1 tbsp	**olive oil**	15 mL
2 cups	**white onions** chopped	500 mL
1 cup	**celery** chopped	250 mL
1 cup	**carrots** chopped	250 mL
1 tsp	**fresh garlic** minced	5 mL
2	**bay leaves**	2
1-1/4 cups	**clam nectar** canned	310 mL
1-1/4 cups	**water** cold	310 mL
1-2 tsp	**fish bouillon**	5-10 mL
2-1/2 cups	**red potatoes** cut into 3/4 inch cubes	625 mL
1/2 cup	**white wine**	125 mL
	equal amounts of whipping cream to base	
1 cup	**scallops**	250 mL
1 cup	**shrimp**	250 mL
1/2 cup	**halibut**	125 mL
1/2 cup	**salmon**	125 mL
1 tbsp	**parsley** chopped	15 mL
1 tbsp	**tarragon**	15 mL

ROUX

1/2 cup	**butter**	125 mL
1/2 cup	**flour**	125 mL
1 tsp	**salt**	5 mL
	fresh pepper to taste	

In a large pot on medium heat add butter and olive oil. Sauté onions, celery, and carrots until onions are clear. Add garlic and bay leaves; cook for 2 minutes. Add remainder of ingredients except whipping cream, this becoming your base. Add hot roux mixture to base. Make sure roux is hot before you add the cold liquid of the clam nectar, water and fish bouillon. Once all liquid is incorporated, add potatoes and cook until the potatoes are soft. If at this point you see the mixture become too thick, add more liquid.

Chef Note

This base can be doubled and frozen for later use. Or, if you wish, you could omit clam nectar and use either vegetable stock or chicken stock. This will allow you to create quite an assortment of cream soups. With a little imagination and a soup pot you can make magic.

Use equal amounts of base to liquid. Therefore, if you have 4 cups of base then you would use 4 cups of whipping cream. Cook on low to medium heat. Stir chowder frequently; it will burn easily if not watched carefully. Bring chowder to a gentle boil to cook the seafood. Do not overcook.

Garnish with chopped parsley and fresh whole baby clams in a shell.

Cucumber & Fennel Salad

Grate 1 tablespoon (15 mL) of zest from the orange and set aside. Cut both ends from the orange, just to the flesh. Set it upright on a chopping board and cut away the pith and skin, following the curve of the fruit. Working over a large bowl, hold the orange in your hand and slide the knife blade down one side of a section, cutting away from the membrane. Cut down the other side of the section and let it fall into the bowl. Continue for the remaining sections, turning back flaps of membrane as you would the pages of a book. Squeeze any remaining juice from the membranes and discard them.

Add the cucumber, fennel bulb, onion and orange zest to the bowl. Mince enough of the fennel fronds to make 2 tablespoons (30 mL) and add it to the bowl. Toss to mix well; chill until ready to serve.

SERVES 8

1	**large navel orange**	1
1	**cucumber** peeled, halved, seeded and thinly sliced	1
1	**fennel bulb** trimmed, cored, quartered and thinly sliced, green fronds reserved	1
1/2	**medium red onion** halved and thinly sliced	1/2

Cucumber & Fennel Salad

Green Springs Crab and Corn Bisque

SERVES 4

1/2 cup	**butter**	125 mL
1/2 cup	**flour**	125 mL
2 cups	**crab stock** see recipe below	500 mL
2	**ears sweet corn** kernels cut off	2
3/4 cup	**whipping cream**	175 mL
1 cup	**lump crab meat**	250 mL
salt and pepper, to taste		
3/4 cup	**green onion** chopped	175 mL

Melt butter in a heavy saucepan; add flour and stir until flour begins to stick to pan. Add crab stock and bring to boil, stirring constantly, then simmer 15 minutes. Add corn kernels and simmer 15 minutes more. Pour in cream and stir well. Gently add crab meat. Remove from heat and let stand 15 minutes for flavors to blend. Reheat gently to serving temperature. Season to taste. Just before serving, add green onions. To hold for serving or to reheat, use a double boiler.

Crab Stock
For crab stock, combine 8 cups (2000 mL) water, 2 medium onions (quartered), and 5 medium-sized hard-shell crabs and cook 45 minutes.

B & W Courtyards Oyster Rockefeller Soup

SERVES 6 – 8

48	**shucked oysters**	48
8 cups	**cold water**	2000 mL
3/4 cup	**butter**	175 mL
1/2 cup	**celery** chopped	125 mL
1/2 cup	**flour**	125 mL
1/3 cup	**Pernod**	75 mL
1 cup	**fresh spinach** **leaves** stemmed and coarsely chopped	250 mL
1/4 cup	**fresh parsley** finely chopped	60 mL
2 cups	**whipping cream**	500 mL
salt and white pepper, to taste		

Place the oysters in a large saucepan and cover with water. Cook over medium heat just until the oysters begin to curl, about 5 minutes. Strain the oysters, reserving the stock; set aside. Melt the butter in a large pot and sauté the celery until tender. Stir in the flour; add the oysters and oyster stock. Reduce the heat and simmer for 10 minutes until thickened. Add Pernod, spinach and parsley; season to taste with salt and pepper. Pour in the whipping cream and simmer several minutes until the soup is hot and ready to serve.

The Gaslight Inn Sweet Red Pepper and Seafood Soup

Sauté peppers, onions, apples, carrots and vegetable oil, stirring frequently, for 5 to 7 minutes, until onions are translucent but not browned. Then add the stock. Bring to a boil over high heat. Reduce heat and simmer, partially covered, for 25 minutes. Puree soup in a blender or food processor fitted with a steel blade. Add red food coloring if desired. Return soup to the saucepan.

Add whipping cream (1 to 3 cups), depending on richness desired and serve warm or chilled. Float a spoonful of sour cream or yogurt in the center and sprinkle with chopped parsley or cilantro leaves.

SERVES 6

4	**large red peppers** seeded, and ribs removed, chopped	4
1/2 cup	**onion** chopped	125 mL
1/4 cup	**apple** peeled, chopped	60 mL
1/4 cup	**carrot** peeled, chopped	60 mL
1 tbsp	**vegetable oil**	15 mL
4 cups	**chicken or vegetable stock**	1000 mL
	sour cream or yogurt	
	parsley or cilantro leaves	

The Gaslight Inn Christmas Seafood Soup

Stir all ingredients into the Sweet Red Pepper Soup base (recipe above) and bring to a boil. Simmer 7 minutes. Another wonderful soup.

SERVES 6 – 8

1/2 cup	**corn kernels** fresh or frozen	125 mL
	pinch crushed hot red pepper	
1/4 cup	**tarragon vinegar**	60 mL
1 tbsp	**freshly squeezed lime juice**	15 mL
2 tbsp	**chopped fresh parsley or cilantro**	30 mL
1/4 tsp	**ground white pepper**	1 mL
1 lb	**small peeled shrimp or calico scallops**	454 g
	salt to taste	

Grilled Salmon Steaks on a Pea Vine Salad

SERVES 4

4	**salmon steaks**	4
	about 8 ounces each	
	salt and freshly ground pepper to taste	
3 tbsp	**olive oil**	45 mL
1-1/2 tbsp	**red wine vinegar**	22.5 mL
1/2 lb	**pea vines**	227 g
	rinsed, tough ends trimmed	

Preheat an outdoor grill. Lightly season the salmon steaks with salt and pepper. While the grill is heating, combine the olive oil and vinegar in a large bowl and whisk to mix. Add the pea vines with salt and pepper to taste. Toss to coat evenly with the dressing. Set aside. When the grill is hot, lightly brush the grate with oil and add the salmon steaks. Cook the fish until just opaque through, 3 to 4 minutes per side.

Arrange the pea vine salad on individual plates and top each with a salmon steak. Serve immediately.

Grilled Salmon Steaks on a Pea Vine Salad

Brierley Hill Fish Chowder

Fry bacon in large pot until brown. Add onions and thyme; sauté about 10 minutes until onions are soft and golden. Add clam juice, potatoes and prawn stock to pot. Bring to a boil, reduce heat and cook covered about 15 minutes until potatoes are done. Add fish and cook another 5 minutes. Add cream, dill, Tabasco®, salt and pepper to taste. Simmer just until heated through. The addition of 1/4 pound (113.5 g) shelled prawns with the fish makes for a special dinner. Garnish with 4 whole prawns sautéed separately in a hot skillet with a little olive oil and butter. Sprinkle parsley over soup.

* When cooking prawns, boil the shells with a bay leaf, some pepper and water to cover for about 20 minutes. Strain and freeze this stock for later use. If you don't have prawn stock on hand, use fish bouillon cubes and water or increase the clam juice by 2 cups (500 mL).

SERVES 4

6	**slices bacon**	6
	diced, fatty ends discarded	
1 cup	**onion**	250 mL
	chopped	
1 tsp	**dried thyme**	5 mL
	or 1 tbsp (15 mL) fresh, chopped	
1-1/2 cups	**clam juice**	375 mL
3	**medium potatoes**	3
	peeled, 1/2-inch cubes	
2 cups	**prawn stock***	500 mL
1 lb	**grouper, snapper**	454 g
	or other firm white fish	
	skinless, boneless, cut into 1-inch pieces	
1 cup	**half & half cream**	250 mL
1 tbsp	**dried dill**	15 mL
	or 2 tbsp (30 mL) fresh	
1/4 tsp	**Tabasco® sauce**	1 mL
	or other hot sauce	
	salt and pepper, to taste	

Seafood Salad

Slice nectarines, peaches and melon. Arrange lettuce leaves in serving dish. Lightly toss prepared cooked seafood, fruit and nuts together. Arrange in serving dish also. Finely dice 1/4 nectarine. Add cream to lime juice and zest. Pour this dressing over the salad or serve separately.

SERVES 4

1/4 cup	**mussel meats**	60 mL
1/4 cup	**prawn tails**	60 mL
1/4 cup	**queen scallops**	60 mL
1/4 cup	**cockles**	60 mL
2	**nectarines**	2
	reserve 1/4 nectarine	
2	**peaches**	2
1	**wedge of melon**	1
3 tbsp	**pine nuts**	45 mL
	selection of lettuce leaves	
1/2 cup	**cream**	125 mL
1	**zest of 1 lime**	1

breakfast & brunch

Salmon does not come cheap. It is not food for every day, but food for the gods, in the same category as Caspian caviar, baby abalone or freshly unearthed truffles.

So eat with the gods. Try a Copper River King. Your palate will think it's in heaven. And don't worry if you feel an urge to swim. It's that old idea that we take on the power of what we eat. In the case of the Copper River King, it might be a long swim. Just go with the flow and smack your lips. You're living on the top of the food chain.

The Seal Beach Inn and Gardens Curry Salmon Quiche

SERVES 4

4	**eggs** beat	4
1-3/4 cups	**half & half cream** enough milk to 2 cup mark	425 mL
6	**green onions** chopped	6
1 cup	**grated cheese** any variety	250 mL
	salt and pepper, to taste	
2 cups	**pink salmon**	500 mL
1 tsp	**curry powder**	5 mL

PASTRY

1 cup	**flour**	250 mL
1/2 cup	**butter**	125 mL
3 tbsp	**cold water**	45 mL

Cut butter into flour. Add iced water 1 tablespoon (15 mL) at a time until dough is moist but not wet. Flour board and roll dough into desired shape. Press into pie plate and flute edges. Preheat oven to 425°F (220°C).

Filling

Chop onions and sauté. Grate cheese, beat eggs, add cream and enough milk to 2 (500 mL) cup mark in a measuring cup. Season with salt, pepper and curry.

Put mixture in pie crust. Drain salmon and take out bones. Chunk salmon, don't flake, and put in base of pie plate. Top with cheese. Add egg and milk mixture. Bake for 15 minutes then reduce heat to 375°F (190°C) and continue to bake for 20 to 25 minutes or until mixture sets firmly.

Salmon Quiche

SERVES 6

1 cup	**salmon** flaked	250 mL
1	**pie crust**	1
3	**large potatoes** thinly sliced	3
2	**eggs**	2
1/2 cup	**milk**	125 mL
2 tbsp	**fresh dill** chopped	30 mL
1 cup	**cottage cheese**	250 mL
1/4 tsp	**salt and pepper**	1 mL

Layer potato slices in piecrust, then add flaked salmon. Mix remaining ingredients in bowl and pour carefully over pie. Bake at 325°F (160°C) for 25 to 30 minutes, or until knife blade comes out clean. Serve at room temperature or chilled.

Quick Pasta Puttanesca

Put 8 cups (2000 mL) of water on to boil in a large pot. Rinse the fish and pat dry; cut it into 1/2-inch cubes. Add the spaghetti to the boiling water; cook, stirring occasionally, until the pasta is al dente, about 8 minutes. While the pasta cooks, combine the capers, anchovies, olives and spaghetti sauce in a medium-size saucepan and bring to a boil, covered over medium heat. Reduce to a simmer and stir in the fish. Simmer and stir gently until the fish flakes when prodded with a fork, about 2 minutes. Drain the pasta and divide among 4 plates. Ladle the sauce over and serve.

SERVES 4

1/3 lb	**cod fillet***	340.5 g
2 tbsp	**capers** chopped	30 mL
2	**anchovy fillets** minced or 2 (10 mL) tsp. anchovy paste	2
1/4 cup	**nicoise, Kalamata** **or ripe black olives** pitted and coarsely chopped	60 mL
1-1/2 cups	**spaghetti sauce**	375 mL
1/8 tsp	**cayenne pepper**	0.5 mL

*other seafood suggestions:
shrimp, squid, clams, mussels, halibut

*Quick Pasta
Puttanesca*

Bethel Point Bed & Breakfast Lobster Omelet

SERVES 6

2 tbsp	**olive oil**	30 mL
1/2	**green pepper** chopped	1/2
1	**small onion** chopped	1
1/2 cup	**mushrooms** chopped	125 mL
3/4 cup	**cooked lobster** cut into small pieces	175 mL
6	**eggs** beaten	6
1/2 tsp	**salt**	2 mL
1/2 tsp	**each of pepper, dill, sage, garlic powder**	1 mL
1/2 cup	**milk**	125 mL
1/2 cup	**cheddar cheese**	125 mL

Pour olive oil into electric skillet and heat to 300°F (150°C). Sauté pepper, onion, mushroom and lobster in olive oil. In medium bowl whisk together eggs, salt, pepper, dill, sage, garlic powder and milk. Remove sautéed mixture from skillet with slotted spoon and place into egg mixture. Pour all ingredients back into skillet and cook 5 minutes. Add cheese and cook for another 5 minutes. Run a narrow spatula around rim of skillet to loosen, lift up and fold omelet onto itself. Cook an additional 2 minutes. Flip onto other side and cook for 2 minutes longer. Cut into servings.

Dockside Guest Quarters York Harbor Stew

SERVES 8

2	**leeks** julienned	2
1 tsp	**saffron** or 1/2 tsp (2 mL) turmeric	5 mL
2 tbsp	**butter**	30 mL
8 cups	**fish stock**	2000 mL
1/4 cup	**Pernod**	60 mL
3 lbs	**boneless, skinned fish pieces or shellfish** any combination, clams, halibut, lobster, mussels, salmon, scallops, shrimp, cod	1350 g
24	**Parisienne potatoes** cooked	24
2	**medium tomatoes** peeled, seeded, diced	2
1/2 cup	**chopped parsley**	125 mL
16	**garlic croutons**	16

Sauté leeks and saffron in butter until tender. Stir in fish stock and Pernod; bring to a boil and reduce heat to simmer. Add fish pieces to stock and simmer just until fish begins to flake, about 5 to 7 minutes. Using a slotted spoon, transfer fish pieces to 8 individual bowls. Add potatoes to each bowl. Top with tomatoes, parsley and croutons.

Poached Salmon with Mustard Sauce

In a small bowl combine the yogurt, mayonnaise, mustard, ginger and honey. Set aside while the fish cooks.

Rinse the salmon in cold water and pat dry with paper towels. Cut the salmon into serving-size pieces. Lay the fish in a single layer in a pan at least 2 inches deep. Add cold water to just cover fish. Lift out the fish and bring the water to a boil. Return the fish to the pan and reduce the heat to keep water just barely simmering (a bubble every 5 to 10 seconds). Simmer until the fish is just slightly translucent in the center, about 8 minutes for fish 1 inch thick. Take the fish from the pan, let drain and pat dry gently with paper towels. Set the fish on plates and spoon the sauce over the top. Garnish with minced chives or parsley.

SERVES 4

2 tbsp	**nonfat plain yogurt or sour cream**	30 mL
1 tbsp	**mayonnaise**	15 mL
1 tsp	**Dijon-style mustard**	15 mL
1/2 tsp	**fresh ginger** minced or grated	2 mL
1/4 tsp	**honey or sugar**	1 mL
1-1/2 lbs	**salmon fillet***	681 g
	minced fresh chives or parsley for garnish	
	*other seafood suggestions swordfish, trout fillets, cod, orange roughy	

Poached Salmon with Mustard Sauce

Open Faced Catfish Sandwich with Jalapeño Tartar Sauce

SERVES 4

4	**slices sourdough bread** thick	4
2 tbsp	**butter or margarine**	30 mL
1-2	**garlic cloves**	1-2
1 cup	**buttermilk**	250 mL
1/2 cup	**flour**	125 mL
1/2 cup	**cornmeal**	125 mL
1 tsp	**cayenne pepper** or to taste	5 mL
1 tsp	**thyme dried**	5 mL
	salt and freshly ground **pepper to taste**	
4	**catfish fillets** about 6 oz. each	4
4 tbsp	**vegetable oil** for frying	60 mL
2 cups	**arugula, escarole** **or other greens** rinsed and dried	500 mL

JALAPEÑO TARTAR SAUCE

1/2 cup	**mayonnaise**	125 mL
1	**jalapeño pepper** cored, seeded and minced	1
1 tbsp	**parsley** minced	15 mL
1 tbsp	**onion** minced	15 mL
1 tbsp	**lemon juice**	15 mL
1 tsp	**prepared horseradish**	5 mL
1/2 tsp	**grated lemon zest**	2 mL
1/4 tsp	**salt**	1 mL

Prepare the tartar sauce by mixing all the ingredients together in a small bowl. Refrigerate until needed.

Toast the sourdough slices, spread lightly with butter and rub them with the whole garlic clove. Cover to keep the toast warm.

Put the buttermilk in a shallow bowl. On a large plate, stir together the flour, cornmeal, cayenne, thyme, salt and pepper. Dip each catfish fillet into the buttermilk, allowing excess to drip off, then thoroughly coat in the flour mixture, patting to remove excess.

Heat the vegetable oil in a large, heavy skillet. Add the catfish fillets and cook over medium-high heat until well browned and just opaque through, about 3 minutes on each side.

Arrange the garlic toast on individual plates and top with the arugula leaves. Set the catfish fillets on the greens and top with a dollop of jalapeño tartar sauce. Serve immediately.

Open Faced Catfish Sandwich with Jalapeño Tartar Sauce

Spring Vegetable and Shrimp Pot with Dill Sauce

In a small bowl stir together the mayonnaise, lemon juice, dill and onion. Let stand at least 20 minutes for flavors to blend.

In a large pot, bring pickling spices and water to a boil. Add the potatoes and simmer uncovered until potatoes are tender when pierced, about 20 minutes. Transfer with a slotted spoon to a large serving platter and cover to keep warm.

While the potatoes cook, devein the shrimp and rinse well, leaving the shells on. Add the shrimp to the boiling water and simmer 1 minute. Add the peas and cook until the shrimp are opaque in the center, about 1 minute more. Drain the shrimp and peas and add to the platter with the potatoes. Serve with dill sauce and/or other sauces to dip vegetables and shrimp into.

SERVES 4

3/4 cup	**low-fat or** regular mayonnaise	175 mL
4 tsp	**lemon juice**	20 mL
1 tbsp	**minced fresh dill** or 1 (5 mL) tsp. dried	15 mL
1 tbsp	**onion** minced	15 mL
3 tbsp	**pickling or** shrimp boil spices optional	45 mL
2 lbs	**small new potatoes** scrubbed	908 g
12 cups	**water** to boil potatoes in	3000 mL
1-1/2 lbs	**medium shrimp***	681 g
1 lb	**sugar snap peas**	454 g

*other seafood suggestions
crawfish, crab legs or whole crab, clams or mussels.

Spring Vegetable and Shrimp Pot with Dill Sauce

Pilgrim's Inn Lobster Chanterelle Mushroom Leek Frittata

SERVES 6

1	**lobster**	1
	1-1/2 pounds	
1 tbsp	**unsalted butter**	15 mL
1	**small leek**	1
	white part only	
1/2 cup	**chanterelle mushrooms**	125 mL
	finely diced	
8	**eggs**	8
2 tbsp	**whipping cream**	30 mL
2 tbsp	**fresh parsley**	30 mL
	chopped	
1 tbsp	**fresh chives**	15 mL
	chopped	
1 tbsp	**fresh chervil**	15 mL
	chopped	
	salt and pepper, to taste	
2 tbsp	**olive oil**	30 mL

Steam or boil the lobster for 10 minutes. Remove from heat and let stand until cool enough to handle. Crack the claws, knuckles and tail section; remove the lobster meat and finely dice. Set aside. Heat the butter in a small sauté pan over medium heat. Add the leek and mushrooms; sauté for 4 to 5 minutes, stirring occasionally. Set aside to cool. Lightly beat the eggs with the cream in a large bowl. Stir in the lobster meat, mushroom mixture and herbs; season with salt and pepper. Heat the olive oil in a 10-inch nonstick skillet over medium heat; pour in the egg-lobster mixture. As the eggs starts to cook, pierce the mixture and pull in the edges with a rubber spatula to allow the uncooked egg on top to move through to the bottom. When the frittata is almost set (firm but still somewhat liquid on top), place the pan under the broiler to finish cooking the top. Slide the frittata onto a cutting board and cut into wedges. Serve hot or at room temperature.

Chef Sutton Scallops in White Wine Sauce with a Hint of Curry

SERVES 2

1 cup	**white wine**	250 mL
1/2 cup	**whipping cream**	125 mL
1 tsp	**curry powder**	5 mL
1/2 tsp	**dried basil flakes**	2 mL
5	scallops	5
	size 10-20, large	
1	**baked puff pastry**	1
	one square for each plate	
	salt and pepper, to taste	

In an 8-inch (20-cm) frying pan, add the wine, curry powder and basil flakes. Reduce by 3/4 volume. Add cream and reduce until it coats a teaspoon. Add salt and pepper to taste. Place the scallops in the saucepan poach for 2 minutes on each side.

Italian Clam and Vegetable Bowl with Toasted Garlic Bread

Put the potatoes in a medium saucepan and add cold water to cover. Bring to a boil and simmer uncovered until the potatoes are tender when pierced with a knife, about 15 minutes. Drain the potatoes and cover to keep warm.

Meanwhile, scrub the clams and discard any that are not tightly closed or that do not close when shells are pressed together. Drain.

In a large pan, heat the oil over medium heat. Add the garlic, onion, basil, oregano, thyme, rosemary and fennel seeds and stir until the onion is tender, about 6 minutes. Quarter the tomatoes, reserving their juice. Add the tomatoes and juice to the pan, cover and bring to a boil.

Add the cooked potatoes, zucchini and beans. Stir in the clams, cover and simmer until the shells open, 5 to 6 minutes. Discard any clams that do not open. Divide the clams, vegetables and broth among 4 large bowls and serve immediately. Pass toasted garlic bread separately.

SERVES 4

3	**medium-sized red skinned potatoes** scrubbed and cut into 3/4-inch cubes	3
2 lbs	**live small hard-shell clams** shells 1-1/2 inches across	908 g
1 tbsp	**olive oil**	15 mL
3	**cloves garlic** pressed or minced	3
1	**small onion** halved and thinly sliced	1
1 tsp	**dry basil leaves**	5 mL
1/2 tsp	**dry oregano**	2 mL
1/2 tsp	**dry thyme**	2 mL
1/2 tsp	**dry rosemary**	2 mL
1/2 tsp	**crushed fennel seeds**	2 mL
4 cups	**whole tomatoes**	1000 mL
1	**small green zucchini** cut into 1/2-inch-thick slices	1
1	**small yellow zucchini or crookneck squash** cut into 1/2-inch thick slices	1
1/4 lb	**fresh green beans or edible pod peas** trimmed	113.5 g

Italian Clam and Vegetable Bowl with Toasted Garlic Bread

Herbed Salmon Mousse Sausages

SERVES 4

2	**large red bell peppers**	2
2 tsp	**balsamic vinegar**	10 mL
1-1/2 lbs	**salmon fillet** skin and pin bones removed	681 g
1	**whole egg or 2 egg whites**	1
1/2 cup	**half & half**	125 mL
	salt and freshly ground **pepper to taste**	
3 tbsp	**chives** minced	45 mL
3 tbsp	**flat-leaf** **(Italian) parsley** minced	45 mL
1 tbsp	**thyme** minced	15 mL
	herb sprigs for garnish	

Preheat the broiler. Roast the bell peppers 4 to 5 inches below the broiler until the skin blackens, turning occasionally to roast evenly, 10 to 15 minutes. Put the peppers in a plastic bag and securely close it. Set aside to cool.

Meanwhile, cut enough of the salmon into fine dice to make 1 cup (250 mL); set aside. Cut the remaining salmon into large chunks, put it in a food processor with the egg and coarsely chop. Add the half & half with a good pinch of salt and pepper and process until fine in texture. Stir in the diced salmon along with half of the chives, parsley and thyme.

Bring a few inches of water to a boil in a large, deep skillet or sauté pan. Add about 1 teaspoon (5 mL) of the mousse mixture and simmer until cooked through, about 1 minute. Taste the mousse, then adjust the seasoning in the remaining mousse if necessary.

Cut 4 pieces of foil about 12 inches long. Lightly brush the foil with oil, leaving 2 inches free on each end. Spoon 1/4 of the salmon mousse down the center of each. Wrap the foil around the mousse to form a cylinder about 1-1/2 inches in diameter, twisting the ends to tighten.

Return the water to a boil. Add the mousse cylinders, lower the heat, to a simmer and poach the "Sausages," uncovered, for 20 minutes.

Meanwhile, finish the sauce. Peel the skin from the roasted peppers and remove the core and seeds. Coarsely chop the peppers and put them in the food processor. Process until smooth, then add the balsamic vinegar and the remaining herbs with the salt and

Herbed Salmon Mousse Sausages

pepper to taste. Spoon the sauce onto 4 plates.

When the salmon sausages are cooked, take them from the pan and carefully unwrap them over the sink (liquid may have accumulated inside the foil). Cut each sausage into 1-inch slices and arrange in a circle over the roasted red pepper sauce. Arrange herb sprigs in the center and serve.

Herbed Salmon Mousse Sausages

Jalapeño Hoe-Cakes with Shrimp Sauce

SERVES 4

1 cup	**corn meal**	250 mL
1-1/2 cups	**water**	375 mL
1/3 cup	**fresh jalapeño peppers** seeded, chopped	75 mL
1 tsp	**salt**	5 mL
1/4 cup	**vegetable oil**	60 mL

SHRIMP SAUCE

2 tbsp	**butter**	30 mL
1/2 cup	**onion** chopped	125 mL
1/2 cup	**green pepper** chopped	125 mL
1 tbsp	**flour**	15 mL
1/2 tsp	**dried summer savory**	2 mL
1/4 tsp	**salt**	1 mL
4	**large tomatoes** peeled, diced	4
1/4 cup	**water**	60 mL
1/2 tsp	**hot pepper sauce**	2 mL
1 lb	**cooked shrimp*** peeled and deveined	454 g

*other seafood suggestions
rock shrimp, spiny lobster
and scallops.

Hoe-Cakes

Combine all ingredients except oil and mix well (the batter will be thin). Add just enough oil in the skillet to cover the bottom and heat to medium-high. Spoon 3 tablespoons (45 mL) of cornmeal mixture in skillet. Cook until edges are browned, turn and cook until brown on the other side. Remove from skillet and drain on absorbent paper. Set aside and keep warm. Serve with shrimp sauce.

Shrimp Sauce

Melt butter in a large skillet over medium heat. Add onion and green pepper and sauté until just tender, 2 to 4 minutes. Stir in flour, savory and salt. Fold in tomatoes, water and hot pepper sauce; cook over low heat, stirring frequently, until sauce is thickened. Add shrimp and heat through. Spoon shrimp sauce over hoe-cakes. Serve immediately.

Barbecued Skate

Heat the oil in a large skillet, add the tomatoes, onion and garlic and cook over medium heat, stirring occasionally, until the onions are translucent, about 5 minutes. Add the molasses, Worcestershire sauce, ginger, and Tabasco sauce, lower the heat to medium and cook uncovered until the vegetables are thoroughly softened and the sauce is thick, 30 to 40 minutes. Take from the heat, stir in the lemon juice and let cool.

Just before serving, cut away any membrane from the skate wings. Preheat the grill or broiler. Brush the skate wings on both sides with some of the cooled barbecue sauce and let sit while the grill heats.

Lightly oil the grill top and add the skate wings. Cook until the fish is nicely browned and somewhat firm, 3 to 4 minutes. Brush the top with some more barbecue sauce, turn the fish and continue cooking until the fish is opaque through, about 4 minutes longer.

Transfer the skate to individual plates, brush with more sauce and serve, passing extra sauce alongside.

SERVES 4

2 lbs	**skinless skate wing** cut in 4 serving portions	908 g

BARBECUE SAUCE

2 tbsp	**vegetable oil**	30 mL
4	**large tomatoes** peeled and chopped	4
1	**onion** minced	1
3	**garlic cloves** minced	3
1/4 cup	**molasses or** **dark brown sugar**	60 mL
1 tbsp	**Worcestershire sauce**	15 mL
1 tbsp	**Tabasco sauce or** **dried red pepper flakes**	15 mL
1/3 cup	**freshly squeezed** **lemon juice**	75 mL

Barbecued Skate

main course

No matter where you live, a clambake makes a great summer party. While traditional clambakes are associated with sand and surf, your kitchen or patio can work just as well. All you need are the right ingredients and some good friends (with big appetites).

The 1661 Inn and Hotel Manisses Oysters Palatine

SERVES 4

2 tbsp	**unsalted butter**	30 mL
4 lbs	**spinach** coarse stems discarded	1816 g
	freshly ground white pepper, to taste	

CURRIED HOLLANDAISE SAUCE

3/4 cup	**unsalted butter**	175 mL
5	**large egg yolks**	5
2 tbsp	**fresh lemon juice**	30 mL
2 tbsp	**dry white wine**	30 mL
2	**dashes Tabasco® pepper sauce**	2
1 tsp	**curry powder** or to taste	5 mL
20	**oysters** shucked, reserving the bottom shells	20

In a large kettle, melt butter over moderately low heat, in it cook the spinach, covered, stirring occasionally for 15 minutes, or until very tender. Drain in a colander. Squeeze out excess liquid from spinach; chop spinach, season it with white pepper and salt. Let spinach cool completely.

Curried Hollandaise

In a small saucepan, heat butter over moderate heat until it is melted and foamy, but do not let it brown. In a blender put yolks, lemon juice, wine, pinch of salt, Tabasco® and turn machine on and immediately off. With the machine at low speed, add the butter in a stream. Cover the blender, increase the speed to high and blend the mixture for 1 minute. Add curry powder and blend sauce well.

Arrange the reserved oyster shells on a large baking sheet, put an oyster in each shell and top with 1 tablespoon (15 mL) of spinach. Bake oysters in the middle of preheated 450°F (230°C) oven for 10 minutes or until heated through. Top each oyster with 1 tablespoon (15 mL) of the curried Hollandaise sauce and broil oysters under a preheated broiler about 4 inches from the heat for 1 minute, or until the tops are browned lightly.

Tipsy Lobster

lobster
butter
whipping cream
wine
Brandy

Heat lobster meat gently in butter. Combine a little wine, brandy and whipping cream; thicken, serve with lobster.

Thai Coconut Milk Curry Sauce with Shrimp

If using the coconut, scatter it in a pie tin or baking pan and bake in a 350°F (175°C) oven, stirring often, until golden, 6 to 8 minutes. Pour into a small bowl and set aside.

Bring 16 cups (4000 mL) of water to a boil in a large pan. Stir in the pasta with 1 (5 mL) teaspoon of salt, if desired. Boil uncovered until tender. While the pasta cooks, combine the coconut milk, fish sauce, brown sugar, cornstarch in a small bowl; set aside. In another bowl combine the basil, mint and green onions; set aside.

Heat the oil in a wok or large frying pan over high heat. Add the ginger and curry paste and stir until fragrant, about 30 seconds. Add the coconut milk mixture and bring to a boil. Add the shrimp and peanuts and simmer until the shrimp is opaque in the center, about 3 minutes. Set aside 3 (45 mL) tablespoons of the basil mixture; gently stir the rest into the sauce along with the lime juice. Put the pasta in a large serving bowl. Pour the seafood and sauce over the pasta and gently toss to coat with sauce. Sprinkle with the toasted coconut and reserved basil mixture and serve.

SERVES 4

1/2 cup	**sweetened shredded coconut** optional	125 mL
1-1/2 cups	**bow tie, gnocchi or shell pasta**	375 mL
1 cup	**unsweetened coconut milk**	250 mL
2 tbsp	**fish sauce, oyster sauce or soy sauce**	30 mL
2 tbsp	**brown sugar**	30 mL
2 tsp	**cornstarch**	10 mL
2/3 cup	**slivered fresh basil leaves**	150 mL
1/3 cup	**slivered fresh mint leaves**	75 mL
2	**green onions** thinly sliced	2
2 tsp	**vegetable oil**	10 mL
2 tbsp	**minced fresh ginger**	30 mL
1 tsp	**Thai red curry paste or Asian chili paste**	5 mL
1 lb	**medium shrimp** peeled and deveined	454 g
1/2 cup	**roasted peanuts or diced red bell pepper**	125 mL
2 tbsp	**fresh lime juice**	30 mL

Baked Salmon with Coarse Sea Salt

2	**salmon fillet pieces*** 6 oz. each	2
1 tbsp	**olive oil**	15 mL
2 tsp	**coarse sea salt**	10 mL
	*other seafood suggestions swordfish, steelhead, bluefish	

Preheat the oven to 375°F (190°C). Rinse the fish under cold water and pat dry with paper towels. Pour the olive oil into a shallow baking dish and add the fillets, turning to coat evenly in the oil. Sprinkle the sea salt over the fillets and bake until just opaque at the center, 10 to 12 minutes.

The Historic Strater Hotel Black Tiger Shrimp Oven-Dried Tomatoes, Spinach Linguine in an Oregano Lobster Broth

SERVES 2 – 3

16	**black tiger shrimp** 16-20 count	16
20	**pieces oven-dried Roma tomatoes**	20
12 oz	**linguine pasta**	375 g
1-1/2 cups	**fresh spinach**	375 mL
4 cups	**lobster broth** recipe below	1000 mL
1 tbsp	**butter**	15 mL
	salt and pepper, to taste	

OREGANO LOBSTER BROTH

1	**onion** chopped	1
1 tbsp	**garlic** chopped	15 mL
1 tsp	**olive oil**	5 mL
2 oz	**white wine**	30 mL
1/2 tbsp	**dry oregano**	7.5 mL
1/2 cup	**lobster meat** drained and added to the broth to make 4 cups broth	125 mL

Sauté onion, garlic, olive oil, white wine and oregano. Keep separate. Steam 4 each of shrimp. Lightly spray 10-inch sauté pan with oil and add onion mixture; add oven-dried tomato pieces. Combine all ingredients in small pot and simmer for 5 minutes, then add to sauté pan. Add shrimp, salt and pepper to taste. Cook linguine in boiling, salted water as directed on package. Add drained pasta to pan. Serve in large pasta bowl. Pull pasta high on the sides of your pasta bowl creating a large hole in the middle for the shrimp. Place the rest of the ingredients into center of ring and pour the remainder of the broth over dish. Top with a small pinch of fried leeks to finish.

Baked Salmon with Coarse Sea Salt

Little St. Simons Island Chef Charles Bostick Shrimp & Tasso Gravy

SERVES 4

5 tbsp	**unsalted butter**	75 mL
1/2 cup	**thinly sliced Tasso ham**	125 mL
1/2 cup	**flour**	125 mL
2 tbsp	**parsley** chopped	30 mL
4 cups	**chicken broth**	1000 mL
2 lbs	**shrimp** peeled, deveined	908 g
1/4 cup	**white wine**	60 mL
salt and pepper, to taste		

Melt 4 tablespoons (60 mL) of the butter over low heat. Sauté the Tasso ham until slightly browned. Dust with flour and make a roux. Sauté for 5 minutes. Then add chicken stock, 2 cups (500 mL) at a time, stirring until well blended. Simmer for 15 minutes. Meanwhile, sauté the shrimp over high heat in remaining 1 tablespoon (15 mL) of butter until almost pink. Add white wine and sauté 1 minute more. Remove from heat and set aside. Add shrimp to Tasso gravy just before serving. Finish with parsley, salt and white pepper to taste.

Maine Lobster Newberg

SERVES 4

2 cups	**cooked lobster**	500 mL
2 tbsp	**butter or margarine**	30 mL
1/4 cup	**sherry**	60 mL
2	**egg yolks** beaten	2
1 cup	**milk**	250 mL
2 tsp	**flour**	10 mL
salt and pepper, to taste		
1/2 cup	**bread crumbs**	125 mL
paprika		

Heat lobster in butter in saucepan for 2 minutes; add sherry. Combine egg yolks, milk and flour and add gradually to lobster. Cook slowly, stirring constantly, until thick. Remove from heat; add salt and pepper. Pour into casserole dish. Sprinkle with paprika. Bake in preheated 350°F (175°C) oven for 35 minutes. Crabmeat or shrimp may be substituted for lobster, if desired.

The Lilac Inn Award-Winning Spicy BBQ Shrimp

Shell the shrimp, leaving tail intact. Make a shallow cut lengthwise down the back of shrimp; wash out and devein. With rubber gloves, remove seeds from pepper and cut into 12 slivers. Make a shallow cut into the underside of each shrimp and insert a piece of pepper. Wrap each shrimp with a bacon strip. Thread 3 bacon/shrimp bundles onto each skewer, leaving a small space between bundles. Baste with barbecue sauce. Grill uncovered over medium coals for 4 to 5 minutes. Turn, baste and grill an additional 4 to 5 minutes or until bacon is crisp and shrimp has turned pink. Serve on a lettuce-lined plate with onion and additional barbecue sauce.

SERVES 2

12	**medium-sized fresh shrimp**	12
1	**small jalapeño pepper**	1
12	**bacon strips**	12
1/2 cup	**barbecue sauce**	125 mL
4	**bamboo skewers** soaked overnight	4
1	**green onion** thinly sliced	1
	additional barbecue sauce	

California Shrimp Scampi

In a medium pan over a low fire, melt 1/4 cup (60 mL) of butter and sauté the garlic and shrimp until the shrimp are firm to touch and lose their translucent appearance. Add the white wine, lemon juice, parsley and return to a simmer. Add the whipping cream and simmer. Reduce heat, add the remaining butter and check the seasoning for salt and pepper. Simmer until the butter melts and sauce thickens. Serve at once over pasta. For a spicier version of this recipe try adding some hot banana pepper rings.

SERVES 2

1 lb	**shrimp** peeled, deveined	454 g
1/2 cup	**butter**	125 mL
2 tbsp	**garlic** chopped	30 mL
1/2 cup	**white wine**	125 mL
2 tsp	**fresh lemon juice**	10 mL
1/4 cup	**whipping cream**	60 mL
	salt and black pepper to taste	
2 tbsp	**fresh parsley** chopped	30 mL
1 lb	**cooked pasta**	454 g

Crab Sauté in Asian Black Bean Sauce

SERVES 2

3 tbsp	**fermented black beans** coarsely chopped	45 mL
1/2 cup	**sake, dry sherry or white wine**	125 mL
3 tbsp	**vegetable oil**	45 mL
2	**whole dried red chilies**	2
1	**red or green bell pepper** cored, seeded and sliced	1
1/2 cup	**snow peas or slender green beans** trimmed	125 mL
1/2 cup	**green onions** sliced	125 mL
1 tbsp	**fresh ginger** minced	15 mL
2 tsp	**garlic** minced or pressed	10 mL
2 lbs	**cooked crab in the shell**	908 g
2 tsp	**cornstarch**	10 mL
1/2 cup	**fish stock, chicken broth or water**	125 mL
1/4 cup	**soy sauce** preferably reduced-sodium	60 mL
1/2 tsp	**dried red pepper flakes, or to taste**	2 mL

Combine the black beans and sake in a small bowl and let sit for at least 30 minutes. Heat the oil in a wok or large skillet over moderately high heat. Add the chilies and cook, stirring, until fragrant and well browned. Remove the chilies and discard them. Add the bell pepper, snow peas, green onions, ginger and garlic to the skillet and stir-fry over high heat until the vegetables are slightly tender, about 3 minutes. Add the crab pieces and toss until heated through, 2 to 3 minutes.

Add the cornstarch to the black beans and sake and stir just to mix. Add this mixture to the wok with the fish stock and soy sauce and stir until the sauce is thickened and evenly coats the crab. Sprinkle with the dried red pepper flakes and taste the sauce for seasoning. Scoop the crab and sauce onto individual plates and serve.

Note

You can use virtually any form of crab for this recipe; whole cleaned Dungeness cut in pieces, sections of snow or King Crab legs, sections of Blue Crab. Be sure to first lightly crack or split leg portions before adding, to make it easier for diners to dig in later. The recipe could even be adapted for soft-shell crabs by first sautéing them separately, then adding them to the stir-fry mixture as you would cooked crab sections.

Cottage on the Cove
Captain Mike's
Steamed Mussels

Cottage on the Cove Captain Mike's Steamed Mussels

In a large pot or wok heat the oil; add minced garlic, onion and spices. When the pan heats to medium-high add the mussels and move them around until they just begin to open. Pour in most of the wine, vinegar and butter. Put the lid on and steam them for about 3 to 4 minutes. When they are all fully opened they are ready to serve into bowls. Serve with slightly crisp garlic bread to soak up the broth.

SERVES 8

6 lbs	**fresh mussels**	2.7 kg
1 cup	**olive oil**	250 mL
1	**head garlic**	1
1	**Walla Walla sweet onion** minced	1
	Tabasco to taste	
	oregano to taste	
	basil to taste	
6	**shakes of red wine vinegar**	6
1/4 cup	**butter**	60 mL
	pepper to taste	
1	**bottle of inexpensive white wine**	750 mL

Three Chimneys Inn Grilled Sea Scallops in Boursin Cheese and Sun-Dried Tomato Sauce

SERVES 4

3 lbs	**jumbo sea scallops** fresh	1.4 kg
1 cup	**champagne vinegar**	250 mL
4 oz.	**Boursin cheese**	112 g
4 tbsp	**whipping cream**	60 mL
	Tabasco® or cayenne pepper to taste	
	squeeze of lemon juice	
4 tbsp	**sun-dried tomatoes**	60 mL
1 cup	**olive oil**	250 mL
	salt and pepper, to taste	
4 tbsp	**shallots** minced sauté in small amount of olive oil	60 mL

Chop up and macerate sun-dried tomatoes in champagne vinegar. Heat gently and set aside to steep in the vinegar. Place cheese in a heavy saucepan. Stir with a wooden spoon to loosen and add heavy cream (sour cream or cream fraiche may be substituted). Pull pot to the side, may need more liquid. Sauté shallots in a small amount of olive oil; set aside. Into a stand-up blender, place sun-dried tomatoes, sautéed shallots, a pinch of salt and pepper. Add olive oil; puree until smooth. Add a few drops of Tabasco or a tiny pinch of cayenne pepper. Add to warm Boursin cheese and cream mixture. Set aside for service. In a smoking hot dry pan, place the scallops that you have seasoned, being sure not to crowd the pan. (otherwise the scallops will boil). Cook about 2-1/2 minutes until they are crusty golden, and not burnt. May need to turn flame down to medium-high heat. Flip over and cook 1 more minute. To serve grilled sea scallops, heat up a touch of the Boursin/sun-dried tomato sauce, add a squeeze of lemon juice and top with scallops, garnish with snipped chives, chervil or chopped parsley. If chive blossoms are in season, they do nicely, as well as do vinegared cucumber or pickled red onion.

York Harbor Inn Lobster-Stuffed Chicken with Boursin Cheese

Sauté onion and celery in clarified butter until limp. Combine with remaining stuffing ingredients. Stuff pounded chicken breasts with 4 tablespoons (60 mL) of stuffing and 4 tablespoons (60 mL) of lobster meat.

Sauce

Bring whipping cream to a boil in a heavy saucepan. Whisk in Boursin cheese and reduce heat to very low. Cook sauce very gently, scraping the bottom of the pan with a rubber spatula often, so that the cheese does not burn. Continue cooking until the sauce is lightly thickened. Sauce may be held for a short time in warm water bath. Bake chicken in a 350°F (175°C) oven for approximately 18 minutes and top with sauce upon serving.

SERVES 8

STUFFING

4 tbsp	**onions** finely diced	60 mL
4 tbsp	**celery** finely diced	60 mL
2 tbsp	**clarified butter**	30 mL
2 tbsp	**dry sherry**	30 mL
1/2 tbsp	**garlic** minced	7.5 mL
1/2 tbsp	**Worcestershire sauce**	7.5 mL
1-1/4 cups	**Ritz crackers** crushed	310 mL
1 tbsp	**scallions** sliced	15 mL
1 tbsp	**parsley** chopped	15 mL
1 tsp	**salt**	5 mL
1 tsp	**white pepper**	5 mL

SAUCE

2 cups	**whipping cream**	500 mL
1-1/4 cups	**Boursin cheese** with garlic and herb	310 mL
8	**6-oz (170-g) boneless skinless chicken breasts** lightly pounded	8
1 lb	**lobster meat** medium diced	454 g

Lobster Mozambique

In a heavy sauté pan, melt the butter and sauté the onion and garlic until they are transparent. Add the lobster meat, clam juice, beer and white wine, then simmer for about 5 minutes. Add chili powder, paprika, salt and pepper. Serve at once over rice.

SERVES 2

1-1/2 cups	**lobster meat** bite-sized chunks	375 mL
2 tbsp	**butter**	30 mL
2 tbsp	**onion** chopped	30 mL
1 tbsp	**garlic** minced	15 mL
1 tsp	**chili powder**	5 mL
1 tsp	**paprika**	5 mL
	salt and pepper, to taste	
1/4 cup	**clam juice**	60 mL
1/4 cup	**beer**	60 mL
1/4 cup	**white wine**	60 mL

Pan-Roasted Sage-Tattooed Atlantic Salmon Filet

SERVES 4

3	**large Yukon gold potatoes**	3
4	**Atlantic salmon fillet pieces** 6 ounces each	4
8	**fresh sage leaves**	8
3 tbsp	**canola oil**	45 mL
	salt and pepper to taste	
2 cups	**field greens or** **other tender lettuce**	500 mL

ROASTED SWEET RED PEPPER
AND SAGE VINAIGRETTE

1 tbsp	**Dijon mustard**	15 mL
1 tbsp	**fresh sage** finely chopped	15 mL
1/4 cup	**roasted sweet** **red pepper**	60 mL
1 tsp	**fresh sage** finely chopped	5 mL
1 tsp	**garlic** finely chopped	5 mL
1/2 cup	**red wine vinegar**	125 mL
1/4 cup	**water**	60 mL
2 tsp	**brown sugar**	10 mL
1/8 tsp	**salt**	0.5 mL
1/8 tsp	**pepper**	0.5 mL
1 cup	**canola oil**	250 mL

To make the dressing

Combine the vinaigrette ingredients (with exception of the oil) in a food processor. Process to blend, then slowly add the oil in a steady stream while the blades are running, to emulsify the sauce. Set aside.

Cut the potatoes into 1/4-inch slices. Bring a large pan of lightly salted water to boil, add the potato slices and simmer just until soft, about 8 minutes. Drain well, then return the potatoes to the warm pan and cover to keep warm.

Preheat the oven to 450°F (230°C) and set the oven rack in the center. Press 2 sage leaves onto the flesh side of each salmon fillet. Season with salt and pepper to taste. Heat a large skillet, preferably non-stick, over medium-high heat. Add the oil and heat until almost smoking. Add the salmon fillets flesh-side down and sear for 2 minutes. If your skillet is not large enough to hold 4 fillet pieces comfortably, sear the salmon in 2 batches.) With all 4 fillet pieces in the skillet, flesh side down, transfer it to the oven and continue cooking until the salmon is just opaque in the center, 3 to 6 minutes longer.

Spoon some of the vinaigrette on individual warmed plates. Place the field greens in the center of each plate and top with the salmon fillet. Surround the salmon with potato coins and drizzle more vinaigrette over if desired.

Pan-Roasted Sage-Tattooed Atlantic Salmon Filet

Camano Island Inn Seafood Stew

Heat oil in heavy pot over medium heat. Add onions and garlic; sauté until onions are tender. Add tomatoes with juices and next 8 ingredients. Bring to boil. Reduce heat and simmer uncovered until liquid is slightly reduced, about 45 minutes. Add clams to pot. Cover pot until clams open, about 10 minutes. Add cod, shrimp and scallops. Simmer until seafood is just cooked through, about 5 minutes. Season to taste with salt and pepper. Garnish with basil.

SERVES 4

1/4 cup	**olive oil**	60 mL
5 cups	**onions** chopped	1250 mL
3 tbsp	**garlic** minced	45 mL
7 cups	**diced tomatoes in juice**	1750 mL
3 cups	**white wine**	750 mL
3 cups	**clam juice**	750 mL
1 cup	**tomato paste**	250 mL
	several bay leaves	
2 tbsp	**chopped fresh thyme**	30 mL
2-1/2 tsp	**grated orange peel**	12 mL
2-1/2 tsp	**fennel seeds** crushed	12 mL
3/4 tsp	**dried crushed red pepper**	4 mL
24	**littleneck clams** scrubbed	24
3 lbs	**cod fillets** cut into 2-inch pieces	1362 g
1-1/2 lbs	**uncooked large shrimp** peeled, deveined	681 g
1 lb	**bay scallops**	454 g
	chopped fresh basil for garnish	

The Cypress Inn Trout with Roasted Pecan Crust

SERVES 4

4	**large Rainbow trout fillets**	4
	salt and pepper, to taste	
	lemon juice, to taste	
1 cup	**fresh bread crumbs**	250 mL
1 cup	**roasted pecans** finely chopped	250 mL
	flour for dredging	
1	**egg** beaten with 2 to 3 teaspoons water	1
1 tbsp	**butter**	15 mL
1 tbsp	**vegetable oil**	15 mL

Season filets with salt, pepper and lemon juice. Let stand at room temperature for 10 to 15 minutes. Combine breadcrumbs and pecans. Dredge fillets in flour, shaking off excess. Dip in egg wash. Place fillets, skin side up, on crumb mixture, pressing into flesh. In large skillet, heat butter and vegetable oil together over medium-high heat. Place fillets, skin side up, in skillet and cook until golden brown, about 3 to 4 minutes; turn and cook 5 to 6 minutes on other side.

Little St. Simons Island Lodge Crab Cakes with Roasted Red Pepper Sauce

SERVES 4 – 6

1 lb	**lump crab meat**	454 g
1	**leek** chopped	1
1/2 cup	**red peppers** or red and yellow combination finely diced	125 mL
1/2 cup	**chopped scallions**	125 mL
1/2 cup	**bread crumbs**	125 mL
1/2 cup	**mayonnaise**	125 mL
1 tbsp	**dried tarragon**	15 mL
2 tbsp	**parsley** chopped	30 mL
1/2 tsp	**hot sauce**	2 mL
1/2 tsp	**salt**	2 mL
1 tsp	**white wine** **Worcestershire sauce**	5 mL
1 tsp	**Dijon mustard**	5 mL
	bread crumbs	
SAUCE		
2–3	**roasted red peppers**	2–3
	balsamic vinegar to taste	
	whipping cream	

Sauce

Roast red peppers in oven 400°F (205°C) until slightly blackened. Return to hot frying pan with a touch of olive oil; add balsamic vinegar and enough whipping cream to create a medium-thick sauce.

Sauté leeks and peppers until tender; add scallions. Combine with remaining ingredients. Adjust seasonings to taste. Form into 1-inch-thick and coat with bread crumbs. Chill until ready to cook. Sauté cakes in a nonstick pan with a minimal amount of oil, approximately three minutes per side. Serve with red pepper sauce or tartar sauce and lemon wedges.

Chef Minnie Giraldi's Shrimp-Stuffed Trout

Preheat oven to 400°F (205°C). At times, boneless, ready-to-stuff trout can be purchased frozen. If the trout are whole, have them boned by the fisherman or fish store. Melt 1 tablespoon (15 mL) of the butter in a small skillet and add 2 tablespoon (30 mL) of shallots and all of the mushrooms. Cook briefly; add chopped shrimp. Stir and cook about 10 seconds. Stir in the 1 tablespoon (15 mL) wine. Spoon and scrape the mixture into a small bowl. Add the breadcrumbs, egg and parsley. Add salt and pepper to taste and blend well. Open up the trout and stuff each with equal portions of the mixture. Tie each trout with a string in two places. Sprinkle the trout with salt and pepper to taste. Butter a shallow baking dish with the remaining butter. Scatter the remaining tablespoon of shallots over it. Arrange the stuffed trout into the dish. Bring the remaining 1/2 cup (125 mL) wine to the boil in a small saucepan on top of the stove, and then pour it around the fish. Place the trout in the oven and bake 15 minutes. Pour the cream around the trout and continue baking about 5 minutes. Baste occasionally with the cream. Remove the string and serve sprinkled with chopped parsley.

SERVES 4

4	**5-oz (155-g) trout** boneless, ready-to-stuff	4
1/2 cup	**white wine**	125 mL
1 tbsp	**white wine**	15 mL
1/2 cup	**fresh bread crumbs**	125 mL
2 tbsp	**butter**	30 mL
1	**egg**	1
3 tbsp	**shallots** finely chopped	45 mL
2 tbsp	**parsley** finely chopped	30 mL
1/2 cup	**mushrooms** thinly sliced	125 mL
	salt and freshly ground pepper	
1/2 lb	**raw shrimp** shelled, deveined and finely chopped	227 g
1/2 cup	**whipping cream**	125 mL
	parsley for garnish	

SERVES 4

8	**sole fillets**	8
1-1/4 cups	**fresh spinach**	310 mL
1	**shallot** minced	1
1	**garlic clove** minced	1
1 tsp	**butter**	5 mL
1/4 cup	**Parmesan cheese**	60 mL
salt and white pepper to taste		
Mornay sauce recipe following		
white wine		

MORNAY SAUCE

2 tbsp	**butter**	30 mL
1/2 cup	**flour**	125 mL
3 cups	**fish stock** simmering	750 mL
1 cup	**whipping cream**	250 mL
	salt to taste	

Fairview Inn Chef McClellan Fillet of Sole à la Florentine with Mornay Sauce

In a skillet, melt butter and cook shallots and garlic. Add spinach and cook until wilted, about 3 minutes. Remove from heat and strain excess liquid. Add cheese and enough Mornay sauce to moisten. (Reserve extra Mornay sauce.) Cool. Divide spinach between fillets and roll into bundles secure with toothpicks. Place on greased baking dish. Sprinkle with wine, salt and pepper. Bake for 15 minutes. Transfer to platter and cover with remaining Mornay sauce.

Sauce

In a saucepan, melt butter. Add flour, stir constantly until paste forms (do not brown). Add fish broth and simmer 5 minutes. Strain sauce into a clean pan and add whipping cream. Simmer for 5 minutes and add pepper and salt to taste.

SERVES 8

8	**6-oz (170-g) salmon fillet**	8
2 tbsp	**butter**	30 mL
lime zest and slices for garnish		

LIME TEQUILA MARINADE

1/2 cup	**olive oil**	125 mL
6 tbsp	**Tequila**	90 mL
2 tbsp	**lime zest**	30 mL
2 tsp	**sugar**	10 mL
6 tbsp	**lime juice**	90 mL
2	**jalapeño peppers** minced	2
2 tsp	**chili powder**	10 mL
1 tsp	**coarse salt**	5 mL

Grilled Tequila Salmon

Mix marinade ingredients in bowl and let stand 1 hour. Marinate salmon in mixture for 1 hour in refrigerator. Drain marinade and set aside. Place salmon skin side down on a large piece of greased foil. Place over low heat on barbecue with lid closed, for about 10 minutes. Brush generously with marinade. Close lid and turn heat to medium. Grill about 15 minutes longer. Meanwhile, boil remaining marinade in heavy saucepan about 5 minutes. Whisk in butter. Drizzle over grilled salmon. Garnish with lime zest and lime slices.

Pan Fried Sole with Tomatoes and Pine Nuts

Preheat the oven to 350°F (175°C) degrees. Put the pine nuts in a shallow baking pan and toast in the oven until lightly browned and aromatic, 5 to 7 minutes. Set aside to cool.

Coat the sole with seasoned flour, patting to remove excess. Heat the olive oil in a large skillet, add the sole and cook over medium heat until nicely browned, 3 to 4 minutes. Carefully turn the fish and continue cooking until just opaque through, about 5 minutes longer. (Less cooking time will be needed for fillets.) Transfer the fish to a platter and cover to keep warm.

Add the tomato, parsley and wine to the skillet and cook over medium-high heat until the sauce lightly thickens, about 2 to 3 minutes. Pour the sauce over the sole, scatter the pine nuts on top and garnish with sprigs of parsley.

Pan Fried Sole with Tomatoes and Pine Nuts

SERVES 2

1/4 cup	**pine nuts**	60 mL
1	**whole sole or small flounder** 1-1/2 – 2 lbs, or 10-12 ounce, sole fillets	1
1/2 cup	**flour** seasoned with salt and pepper	125 mL
3 tbsp	**olive oil**	45 mL
1 cup	**diced tomato**	250 mL
1/4 cup	**chopped parsley**	60 mL
1/4 cup	**white wine or freshly squeezed lemon**	60 mL
	parsley sprigs for garnish	

Rabbit Hill Inn Baked Ginger Snap Crusted Chilean Sea Bass

SERVES 2

2-7 oz.	**portions Sea Bass** **or any firm white fish**	2-196 g

GINGER SNAP CRUMBS

3/4 cups	**butter** softened	175 mL
1 cup	**sugar**	250 mL
3 tbsp	**molasses**	45 mL
1	**egg**	1
2-1/4 cups	**flour** sifted	560 mL
3/4 tbsp	**ginger** ground	4 mL
3/4 tbsp	**cinnamon** ground	4 mL
2 tsp	**baking soda**	10 mL

KIWI LIME SAUCE

1 cup	**white wine**	250 mL
1/2 tbsp	**shallots** minced	7.5 mL
2 tbsp	**fresh ginger** minced	30 mL
8	**kiwis** peeled	8
2/3 cup	**fresh lime juice**	150 mL
1/4 cup	**honey**	60 mL

Dredge bass in crumbs; coat on both sides. Bake at 350°F (175°C) degrees for 12 to 15 minutes or until firm. Serve with Kiwi Lime Sauce.

Ginger Snap Crumbs

Cream together butter, sugar, molasses, and egg until light and fluffy. Combine dry ingredients and gently stir into the mix. Form dough into small ball shapes. Bake at 325°F (160°C) oven for 12 to 15 minutes. Remove from oven and let cool. Puree cookies into a fine meal in the food processor. (You can use purchased ginger snap cookies, but it is worth the time to make these delicious cookies).

Kiwi Lime Sauce

Combine white wine, shallots and ginger in saucepan and bring to boil. Reduce mixture down by half. Add kiwis, lime juice and honey to mixture in saucepan and simmer for 15 minutes. Remove from heat and puree in food processor. Strain.

Crab Quiche

SERVES 6

1/2 cup	**mayonnaise**	125 mL
2 tbsp	**flour**	30 mL
2	**eggs** beaten	2
1/2 cup	**milk**	125 mL
1 cup	**crab meat**	250 mL
1 cup	**Swiss cheese** diced	250 mL
1/2 cup	**green onion** chopped	125 mL
1	**unbaked 8-inch pie shell**	1

Combine mayonnaise, flour, eggs and milk in bowl; mix until well blended. Stir in crabmeat, cheese and onions; pour into pie shell. Bake in preheated 350°F (175°C) oven for 40 to 45 minutes or until knife inserted in center comes out clean.

Three Chimneys Inn Grilled Rainbow Trout in Grape Leaves

Bring the unsalted butter to room temperature. With a fork, mix in capers, salt and pepper. Apply evenly but not liberally to the top of each trout fillet. Add two sprigs of dill to the top of each of the buttered fillets. Wrap each fillet tightly with 4 of the wine-poached grape leaves then refrigerate for approximately 30 minutes. Pan roast two medium yellow tomatoes in a light amount of olive oil until lightly browned then remove skin and seeds. Repeat the process with the garlic. Puree the sauce ingredients together in a blender then refrigerate. On a preheated grill, cook the trout fillets approximately 4 minutes on each side or until the meat is tender and flaky.

SERVES 4

4-5 oz.	**Rainbow trout fillets** with pinbones removed	4-112 g
4 tsp	**capers** crushed and minced	20 mL
4 tsp	**unsalted butter** whipped	20 mL
8	**sprigs of fresh dill**	8
	salt and pepper, to taste	
16	**steamed grape leaves** poached in a little wine (can be purchased in jars, then rinsed)	16

SAUCE: YELLOW TOMATO COULIS WITH PAPAYA

2	**roasted yellow tomatoes** 2 per person	2
1 tsp	**roasted garlic**	5 mL
1/2	**papaya** peeled, seeded	1/2

Ginger–Sesame Salmon

Arrange hot salmon in a single layer on a serving platter. Stir together the soy sauce, seasoned rice vinegar and ginger and spoon over salmon. Cut green onions into 1-inch lengths, then slice each piece into very thin strips; scatter over salmon. In a small saucepan combine garlic and sesame oil. Warm mixture, stirring over medium heat until garlic turns golden. Immediately drizzle oil mixture over salmon.

SERVES 2

1 lb	**hot grilled baked or broiled salmon**	454 g
2 tsp	**soy sauce**	10 mL
2 tsp	**seasoned rice vinegar**	10 mL
1 tbsp	**fresh ginger** minced or grated	15 mL
2	**green onions** ends trimmed	2
1	**clove garlic** minced or pressed	1
1 tbsp	**sesame oil**	15 mL

Steamed Mussels & New Potatoes with Rosemary & Roasted Garlic Sabayon

SERVES 4

1-1/2 lbs	**small new red potatoes**	681 g
1 tbsp	**white vinegar**	15 mL
2 lbs	**mussels** scrubbed and de-bearded	908 g
1/2 cup	**white wine** more if needed	125 mL
4	**3-inch sprigs fresh rosemary**	4
5	**egg yolks**	5
1-1/2 tbsp	**roasted garlic paste**	22.5 mL
1/2 tsp	**salt**	2 mL
1/2 tsp	**ground black pepper**	2 mL
1	**juice of 1 lemon**	1
rosemary sprigs and blossoms if available, for garnish		

Chef's Note

To make garlic paste, bake whole heads of garlic (wrapped in foil) at 400°F (205°C) for 45 minutes. Let cool slightly, then separate the cloves, squeeze out the tender garlic and mash it with a fork in a small bowl. One large head of garlic will roughly yield the roasted garlic needed in this recipe.

Wash the potatoes and cut them in half if they are larger than a walnut. Fill a large pot with cool salted water and add the potatoes and vinegar. Bring to a boil over high heat, then reduce the heat to a low boil and continue to cook until tender, about 10 minutes. Drain and keep the potatoes warm.

Put the mussels, wine and rosemary in a large pan and cover tightly. Set the pan over high heat and steam just until the mussels open, about 3 to 4 minutes. Transfer the mussels to a large bowl and cover to keep warm; discard any mussels that do not open. Pour the mussel nectar from the pan through a fine sieve; discard the rosemary sprigs. Also strain any mussel nectar that has collected in the bottom of the bowl. Measure 1-1/2 cups (375 mL) of nectar, adding white wine if there is not enough nectar.

Combine the egg yolks, roasted garlic paste, salt and pepper in a medium stainless steel bowl and whisk until smooth. Add the measured mussel nectar with the lemon juice. Set the bowl on top of a saucepan of boiling water (the water should not touch the bottom of the bowl).

Steamed Mussels & New Potatoes with Rosemary & Roasted Garlic Sabayon

Whisk vigorously until the sabayon is frothy and thickened and there is no trace of liquid at the bottom of the bowl, about 3 to 5 minutes.

Put the potatoes in the middle of four large, shallow soup plates. Arrange the mussels, hinge-down, in a circle around the potatoes. Spoon the sabayon over the mussels and potatoes. Sprinkle with rosemary blossoms, if available, and serve immediately.

Steamed Mussels & New Potatoes with Rosemary & Roasted Garlic Sabayon

Oysters with Champagne Sauce

SERVES 4

20	**oysters**	20
	shucked	
1	**recipe of Champagne sauce**	1
1/4 cup	**thin-sliced prosciutto**	60 mL
	julienned	
1/4 cup	**pistachio nuts**	60 mL
	chopped	
4	**fresh parsley sprigs**	4

CHAMPAGNE SAUCE

1 tbsp	**minced shallot**	15 mL
1/2 cup	**dry Champagne**	125 mL
4 tbsp	**unsalted butter**	60 mL
	cut in small pieces	
2 tbsp	**Champagne vinegar**	30 mL
	salt and white pepper, to taste	
1 cup	**whipping cream**	250 mL

Preheat the oven to 450°F (230°C). Place the oysters on a baking sheet and bake them for 2 to 4 minutes or until the edges of the oysters begin to curl. Spoon the champagne sauce over the oysters and top the oysters with the prosciutto and pistachios. Return the oysters to the oven for 45 seconds to warm the sauce. To serve, place a bed of rock salt on each of the dishes and arrange 5 oysters in half shells on each plate. Garnish with sprig of fresh parsley.

Place the shallot, Champagne and vinegar in a small saucepan over medium heat. Bring to a boil and cook to reduce by a third. Add the cream to the pan; cook to reduce again by one third. Remove the pan from heat but keep the burner on low. Whisk in the butter one piece at a time. Return the pot to the burner for a few seconds if the sauce cools too much to melt the butter. Season the sauce with salt and pepper, adding a minimum of salt since the prosciutto is salty. Strain the sauce through a fine mesh sieve and keep it warm over hot water. The sauce may be made up to 2 hours in advance and poured into a warm thermos.

SERVES 4

1 lb	**salmon**	454 g

MARINADE

3/4 cup	**bourbon**	175 mL
2 tbsp	**honey**	30 mL
1/2 tsp	**ginger**	2 mL
1/2 cup	**brown sugar**	125 mL
2 tsp	**soy sauce**	10 mL
	pepper, to taste	

Sous Chef Nina Rossini Honey Bourbon Salmon

Combine marinade ingredients and pour over salmon. Marinate for 1 hour. Spray grill with cooking spray. Grill salmon for 4 minutes on each side.

Killer Baked Oysters

In microwave, melt butter and margarine. Put all ingredients except oysters, bacon and cheese into a blender and puree. Shuck oysters over a baking tray and pour any juice from the oysters into the blender and mix again. Put oysters on the larger half of the shell, then place on baking tray. Pour sauce from blender over each oyster; top each oyster with crumbled bacon and grated cheese. Bake in oven at 400°F (205°C) for 5 to 10 minutes, or until the mixture begins to bubble. Serve immediately.

SERVES 4

1/2 cup	**butter**	125 mL
1/2 cup	**margarine**	125 mL
1/2 cup	**cooked spinach**	125 mL
1/2 cup	**cooked mustard greens**	125 mL
1/4 cup	**fresh parsley** minced	60 mL
1/4 cup	**celery** minced	60 mL
1/2 cup	**onion**	125 mL
6	**garlic cloves**	6
1/2 tsp	**hot sauce**	2 mL
1/2 tsp	**salt**	2 mL
3	**dozen oysters in the shell**	3
5	**strips bacon** cooked and crumbled	5
1/2 cup	**Gruyere cheese** grated	125 mL

Oysters Rockefeller

Preheat the oven to 450°F (230°C). Shuck oysters. Leave oysters in deep half of shell. Fry bacon until slightly crisp, drain on paper towels. Chop bacon finely and set aside.

Sauté celery, onion and parsley in margarine until slightly tender. Remove sautéed vegetables from stove; add spinach and anisette. Line baking trays with rock salt, 1/4-inch deep. Place oysters in shells in rock salt and pack down. Sprinkle 1 teaspoon (5 mL) spinach mixture over each oyster. Sprinkle 1/2 teaspoon (2 mL) finely chopped bacon over each. Melt 1-1/2 tablespoons (7.5 mL) margarine and mix in bread crumbs. Sprinkle lightly on oysters. Bake for 10 minutes and serve.

SERVES 4

20	**oysters** in shell	20
8	**bacon strips**	8
4 tbsp	**margarine**	60 mL
4 tbsp	**celery** chopped fine	60 mL
4 tbsp	**onions** chopped fine	60 mL
2 tbsp	**parsley** chopped	30 mL
1 cup	**spinach** chopped, thawed and well drained	250 mL
1 tbsp	**anisette** optional	30 mL
1-1/2 tbsp	**margarine**	22.5 mL
2 tbsp	**bread crumbs**	30 mL
	rock salt	

Pan Fried Peppered Halibut with Pears and Watercress

SERVES 4

2	**medium-size ripe pears** cored and thinly sliced	2
3/4 cup	**watercress** rinsed, tough stems removed	175 mL
4	**halibut fillet pieces**	4
1 tbsp	**black peppercorns**	15 mL
2 tbsp	**olive oil**	30 mL
1 cup	**pear juice or apple juice**	250 mL
2 tsp	**red or white wine vinegar**	10 mL

Combine the pear slices and watercress in a large bowl. Rinse the halibut, pat dry with paper towels and lay it on a plate, skin side down. Crush the peppercorns with a mortar and pestle. Press the crushed pepper evenly on to the halibut.

In a medium skillet, heat the olive oil over medium heat. When hot, add the halibut skin side up. Cook for 3 to 4 minutes, turn the fish and continue cooking until the fish is just opaque in the center, 3 minutes longer. (If the halibut is thick and not yet cooked through, lower the heat, cover the pan and continue cooking for a few minutes.) Transfer the fish to a plate and cover with foil to keep warm.

Add the pear juice to the skillet, increase the heat to medium high and cook until reduced by about half, 5 to 7 minutes, stirring occasionally and incorporating bits of fish and pepper from the bottom of the pan. Turn off the heat and stir in the vinegar. Pour the hot mixture over the pears and watercress and toss to evenly coat. Divide the pears and watercress among individual plates, set a piece of fish on top and drizzle the fish with the juices remaining in the bowl.

Pan Fried Peppered Halibut with Pears & Watercress

Shrimp à la Bordelaise

In a medium pan over a low fire, heat half the butter and the olive oil; sauté the garlic, shallots and shrimp until the shrimp are firm to touch and lose their translucent appearance. Add the white wine, scallions, parsley and return to a simmer. Add whipping cream, red pepper and return to a simmer. Reduce heat, add the remaining butter and adjust the seasoning. Simmer until the butter melts and sauce thickens. Serve at once over your favorite pasta. Garnish with chopped parsley and lemon wedge.

SERVES 2

1 lb	**shrimp** peeled, deveined shrimp	454 g
2 tbsp	**olive oil**	30 mL
6 tbsp	**butter**	90 mL
2 tbsp	**shallots**	30 mL
1 tbsp	**garlic** chopped	15 mL
4 tbsp	**scallions** chopped	60 mL
1/2 cup	**Chardonnay** dry white wine	125 mL
2 tbsp	**fresh parsley** chopped	30 mL
1/4 cup	**whipping cream**	60 mL
	pinch crushed red pepper	
	salt and black pepper, to taste	
1 lb	**cooked pasta**	454 g

Boiling Lobster Tails

SERVES 4

5 lbs	**live lobsters**	2.5 k g
	or thawed frozen lobster tails	
2 tsp	**salt**	10 mL
	for each quart of water	

Pour enough water into a large pot to generously cover 5 lbs of live lobsters or thawed frozen lobster tails. Add 2 teaspoons (10 mL) salt, if desired, for each quart of water. Bring to a boil over high heat. Add lobster tails or plunge live lobsters head first into water, tucking tails under to prevent splashing. Cover pot. When water resumes boiling, reduce heat and simmer according to chart below or until meat is opaque when cut.

Grilling Lobster Tails

Thaw lobster tails, they will be more tender than if cooked frozen. Insert point of kitchen shears between meat and hard shell on back. Clip shell down center, leaving fantail intact. Do not remove underside membrane. Gently open shell, separating it from the meat. Lift raw tail meat through split shell. Arrange lobster tails, membrane side up in shallow pan with a small amount of water in bottom of pan to prevent drying. Broil on grill 4 inches from heat regardless of size. Turn, brush with melted butter and broil on grill according to chart.

Time Table for Broiling and Boiling Lobster Tails

Weight	1–3 oz.	4–6 oz.	10–12 oz.	14–16 oz.
Broiling	3–4 min.	5–6 min.	8–10 min.	12–15 min.
Boiling	3–5 min.	5–7 min.	10–12 min.	15–20 min.

Halibut with Vegetable Confetti

Lightly season the halibut fillets with salt and pepper. Heat olive oil in skillet and sauté halibut until golden on both sides and fish is opaque in center. Remove fillets from pan and set aside on heated serving plates.

Add diced leek, red pepper, asparagus, celery and carrot to the pan and sauté on high heat about 30 seconds. Add wine and butter to the vegetable mixture and continue sautéing while moving the pan back and forth to prevent scorching. Continue sautéing until a sauce is formed, about 1 to 2 minutes. Spoon the sauce around the halibut on each plate. Garnish with a sprinkle of chopped chives and a dollop of caviar (optional) on top of each fillet.

SERVES 2

2	**fresh halibut fillets** 3-4 ounces (85-125 g)	2
	salt and pepper to taste	
1 tbsp	**olive oil**	15 mL

VEGETABLE CONFETTI

1/4 cup	**leek** diced	60 mL
1/4 cup	**sweet red pepper** diced	60 mL
1/4 cup	**asparagus or zucchini** diced	60 mL
2 tbsp	**carrot** diced	30 mL
2 tbsp	**celery** diced	30 mL
1/2 cup	**dry white wine**	125 mL
2 tsp	**butter**	10 mL

GARNISH

2 tsp	**chives** chopped	10 mL
1 tsp	**caviar**	5 mL

Clams Casino

Place each clam on a washed shell. Add green pepper, tomato sauce, cheese and bacon in that order. Broil until bacon is crisp.

SERVES 4 – 6

12	**clams** opened on shell	12
1 cup	**green pepper** chopped	250 mL
2 cups	**tomato sauce or spaghetti sauce**	500 mL
	Parmesan cheese	
4	**strips of bacon** divide each strip into 3 pieces	4

Jamaican Orange Sea Bass

Jamaican Orange
Sea Bass

SERVES 4

2 tbsp	**allspice berries**	30 mL
2	**jalapeño or Serrano chilies** cored, seeded and minced, more or less to taste	2
3	**cloves garlic** minced or pressed	3
3	**green onions** minced	3
1/4 cup	**freshly squeezed** **orange juice**	60 mL
1 tbsp	**grated orange zest**	15 mL
1 tbsp	**vegetable oil**	15 mL
	salt and pepper to taste	
2 lbs	**sea bass fillets** cut in serving portions	908 g
2	**navel oranges** cut in 1-inch slices	2

Finely crush the allspice berries with a mortar and pestle, or grind them in a spice grinder. In a small bowl, combine the allspice with the chilies, garlic, onions, orange juice, orange zest, oil, salt and pepper. Stir to mix well. Preheat the grill. Set the sea bass fillets in a shallow dish and lightly spoon the marinade mixture over. Turn the fillets so they are evenly coated in the marinade and set aside for 10 to 15 minutes (chill if the ambient temperature is quite warm).

Put the fish fillets on the hot grill, with the orange slices alongside. Cook until the fish is just opaque through, 3 to 4 minutes per side. Turn the orange slices occasionally, so they brown evenly. Serve the grilled sea bass with grilled orange slices alongside.

Poached Salmon in Champagne Sauce

Gently poach salmon portions in simmering water with salt, pepper and bay leaf for 4 to 6 minutes.

Sauce

Melt butter and cook shallots and onion until translucent. Add lemon juice, champagne and cider vinegar. Bring to boil and simmer until liquid is reduced to 1/3. Add cream and simmer gently for 10 to 15 minutes. Check seasoning.

Arrange alternate layers of pancakes and salmon on plates. Top with cooked buttered ribbons of leek and carrot. Serve with champagne sauce on warm plates.

SERVES 4

1-1/2 lbs	**salmon** cut into 8 rounds	708 g
8	**small light pancakes or crepes**	8
salt and freshly milled pepper		
1	**bay leaf**	1
1	**carrot** julienne	1
1	**leek** julienne	1

SAUCE

6 tbsp	**shallots or onion** diced	90 mL
3 tbsp	**lemon juice**	45 mL
1/2 cup	**champagne**	125 mL
2 tbsp	**cider vinegar**	30 mL
1/2 cup	**whipping cream**	125 mL
	knob of butter	

Grilled Tuna with Pineapple-Ginger Marinade

Combine pineapple juice, vinegar, soy sauce, ginger, oil and garlic in a small bowl; mix well. Arrange tuna in glass or ceramic baking dish. Pour marinade over fish. Marinate in refrigerator, covered, at least 30 minutes. Drain fish, reserving marinade. Place fish on oiled grill 4 to 5 inches from hot coals. Barbecue 6 minutes per inch of fish measured at its thickest point, basting frequently. Turn fish halfway through cooking time. Tuna should be pink in the center when removed from heat. Garnish with green onions, if desired.

SERVES 4

1/4 cup	**pineapple juice**	60 mL
2 tbsp	**rice wine vinegar**	30 mL
1 tsp	**salt-reduced soy sauce**	5 mL
1 tsp	**fresh ginger** grated	5 mL
2 tsp	**vegetable oil**	10 mL
1 tsp	**garlic** minced	5 mL
4	**tuna steaks**	4
2	**green onions** diagonally sliced (optional)	2

Halibut with Lentils and Greens

SERVES 2

3/4 cup	**lentils**	175 mL
1-3/4 cup	**reduced-sodium chicken broth**	425 mL
1/2 cup	**water** more if needed	125 mL
4	**sprigs fresh thyme** or 1 teaspoon (5 mL) dried	4
1	**bay leaf**	1
1/3 lb	**hardy greens (mustard, kale, turnip)** rinsed and tough stalks removed	150 g
2	**halibut steaks** 6-8 oz. each	2
	pinch ground cloves	
	salt and pepper to taste	
2 tsp	**vegetable oil**	10 mL
1/2 cup	**dry red wine**	125 mL

Put the lentils in a medium saucepan with the chicken broth, water, thyme and bay leaf. Bring to a boil, then lower the heat and simmer until the lentils are just tender, 15 to 20 minutes. Add a little more water during cooking if necessary to keep the lentils covered with liquid. Drain the lentils and set aside.

Stack the greens and loosely roll up the leaves, then cut across into about 1-inch strips.

Rinse the halibut in cold water and pat dry with paper towels. Season the fish with a pinch of cloves, salt and pepper. Heat the oil in a heavy-bottomed skillet, preferably non-stick. Add the halibut and cook over medium-high heat until browned, about 5 minutes. Turn the halibut and continue cooking until the fish is opaque through the thickest part, 3 to 5 minutes longer. Transfer the fish to warmed plates and cover to keep warm.

Add the red wine to the skillet, bring to a boil and boil for 1 minute. Add the shredded greens and cook over high heat, stirring, until the greens are wilted. Add the lentils and toss just until heated. Season to taste with a pinch of cloves, salt and pepper. Spoon the lentil mixture over and alongside the halibut steaks and serve.

Chef notes

Common brown lentils are perfectly suited for this recipe, but you can also use other varieties, such as red or green. Other lentils may require different cooking times, however, so note package instructions before cooking.

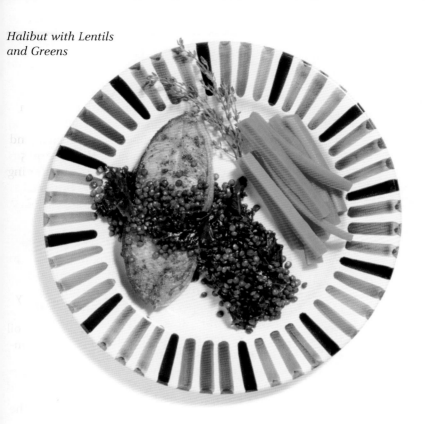

Halibut with Lentils and Greens

Burgers from the Sea

Combine all ingredients in medium bowl. Divide into equal portions, shape into patties. Heat the barbecue grill until the coals glow red with white ash around the edge. The salmon patties are fragile, so handle them carefully; if you chill the patties on a plate in the refrigerator before putting them on the grill they will hold together better.

Grill until desired doneness.

SERVES 4

1 lb	**boneless, skinless salmon fillet** well chopped	454 g
2 tbsp	**bread crumbs**	30 mL
1 tbsp	**Dijon mustard**	15 mL
1 tbsp	**onion** minced	15 mL
2 tsp	**lemon juice**	10 mL
1/2 tsp	**garlic** minced	2 mL
1/2 tsp	**ground black pepper**	2 mL
1/2 tsp	**salt**	2 mL

Chilean Sea Bass a La Grecque

SERVES 4 – 6

1-1/2 lbs	**Chilean sea bass fillet**	681 g
bones removed, cut in serving pieces		
salt and pepper to taste		
1/4 cup	**flour** more if needed	60 mL
2 tbsp	**olive oil**	30 mL
1	**small onion** minced	1
3-4	**cloves garlic** minced or pressed	3-4
1-1/2 lbs	**tomatoes** chopped	681 g
1/4 cup	**lemon juice**	60 mL
2	**bay leaves**	2
1 tsp	**dry rosemary** crushed	5 mL
1 tsp	**dry oregano**	5 mL
1/2 tsp	**coriander seeds** or ground coriander	2 mL

Rinse the Chilean sea bass with cold water and pat dry with paper towels. Lightly season the fish with salt and pepper, then coat with flour, shaking off the excess. Heat the oil in a skillet over medium-high heat, add the fish pieces and cook just until lightly browned, about 1 minute on each side. Transfer to a plate and set aside.

Add the onion and garlic to the skillet and cook, stirring, until beginning to soften, 1 to 2 minutes. Add the tomatoes, lemon juice, bay leaves, rosemary, oregano, coriander, salt and pepper and cook over high heat, stirring, for 3 to 4 minutes. Add the fish pieces and press them gently into the tomato mixture, cover the skillet and cook over medium heat until the fish is no longer opaque in the center, 8 to 10 minutes. Discard the bay leaves, transfer the fish and tomato mixture to warmed dinner plates and serve with rice or pasta.

Chilean Sea Bass a La Grecque

Warm Bean Salad with Smoked Whitefish and Greens

Warm Bean Salad with Smoked Whitefish and Greens

Soak the beans in cold water to cover overnight. Drain the beans, put them in a saucepan and add 4 cups (1000 mL) fresh cold water. Cook the beans over medium-high heat until just tender, about 35 minutes. Drain well and set aside. Heat the oil in a large pan, add the garlic and sauté until aromatic. Add the cooked beans and bread-crumbs and continue to cook, stirring regularly, until the beans are lightly coated and the crumbs begin to brown, about 3 minutes. Add the flaked fish, greens, tomato, vinegar, salt and pepper. Sauté until the greens are lightly wilted, about 2 minutes and serve.

SERVES 2

1 cup	**great northern beans**	250 mL
	or use flageolets, baby limas or other firm beans	
4 cups	**cold water** to cook beans	1000 mL
2 tbsp	**olive oil**	30 mL
3	**cloves of garlic** minced or pressed	3
1 cup	**dry bread crumbs**	250 mL
1/2 lb	**smoked whitefish** skin and bones removed, coarsely flaked	227 g
3 cups	**cleaned, torn greens such as spinach, kale, escarole or chard**	750 mL
1 cup	**diced tomato**	250 mL
2-1/2 tbsp	**red wine or sherry vinegar**	37.5 mL
	salt and pepper, to taste	

Sesame Poppy Mahimahi with Pineapple Sauce

SERVES 4

4	**mahimahi fillet pieces**	4
	7-8 oz. each	
2 tsp	**sesame oil**	10 mL
	salt and pepper to taste	
2 tbsp	**poppy seeds**	30 mL
2 tbsp	**white sesame seeds**	30 mL
2-3 tsp	**vegetable oil**	10-15 mL

PINEAPPLE SAUCE

2 cups	**pineapple**	500 mL
	coarsely chopped fresh or drained, canned	
1 cup	**orange juice**	250 mL
1 tbsp	**fresh ginger**	15 mL
	minced or grated	
	pinch dried red pepper flakes	
	optional	

To make the chunky pineapple sauce, combine the pineapple, orange juice, ginger and dried red pepper flakes in a small heavy saucepan. Bring just to a boil and gently boil over medium-high heat until the liquid is reduced by about 3/4 and the sauce is slightly thickened, 15 to 20 minutes.

Meanwhile, prepare the mahimahi. Rub each fillet piece with 1/2 teaspoon (2 mL) of the sesame oil and season with salt and pepper to taste. Set the mahimahi pieces on a plate and sprinkle half of each fillet surface with poppy seeds. Sprinkle the other half of the fillets with sesame seeds. (For tidy lines, lay a piece of paper across half of the fillet piece and sprinkle seeds over the exposed portion; then lay the paper over the first seeded sectioned and sprinkle the other seeds over.) Press gently with your fingers to help the seeds adhere.

Heat the vegetable oil in a large skillet, preferably non-stick. Add the fillet pieces seeded-side down and sauté over medium heat until lightly colored, 3 to 4 minutes. Carefully turn the fillets and continue cooking until just opaque through, 3 to 5 minutes longer.

Arrange the mahimahi fillets on individual plates. Spoon the sauce over and around the mahimahi and serve.

Chef Notes
For extra simplicity, use only sesame or poppy seeds rather than both. And you can also use your favorite fruit salsa or other tropical-style sauce in place of the pineapple sauce.

*Sesame Poppy Mahimahi with
Pineapple Sauce*

Lobster Alfredo

In a medium sauté pan, melt the butter and
sauté the garlic until it begins to brown.
Add the white wine and the clam juice and
bring the sauce to a simmer. Reduce the heat
and add the lobster meat. Simmer for 10
minutes or until lobster meat is hot. Add
the whipping cream and butter; simmer
until the butter melts and the sauce begins
to thicken. Add the cheese, salt and pepper.
Serve at once over cooked pasta. Garnish
with chopped parsley.

SERVES 2

1-1/2 cups	**cooked lobster meat**	375 mL
2 tsp	**garlic** chopped	10 mL
4-6 cups	**whipping cream**	1000-1500 mL
1/4 cup	**white wine**	60 mL
1/4 cup	**butter** depending on thickness	60 mL
1/2 cup	**Parmesan cheese**	125 mL
	clam juice, to taste	
	salt and pepper, to taste	
	chopped parsley	
1 lb	**cooked pasta**	454 g

Red Currant Glazed Salmon with Couscous Salad

SERVES 4

1	**medium zucchini**	1
	cut in 1/2-inch dice	
1	**large carrot**	1
	cut in 1/2-inch dice	
1 cup	**couscous**	250 mL
1 cup	**chicken broth or water**	250 mL
2 tbsp	**basil**	30 mL
	minced	
1 tbsp	**olive oil**	15 mL
salt and freshly ground pepper		
1/4 cup	**red currant jelly**	60 mL
4	**salmon fillet pieces or steaks**	4
	about 6 oz. each	

Preheat an outdoor grill or preheat oven to 400°F (205°C) degrees. Bring a small pan of lightly salted water to a boil. Add the zucchini and boil until just tender, 1 to 2 minutes. Scoop out the zucchini with a slotted spoon and drain. Return the water to a boil, add the carrot and boil until just tender, 3 to 4 minutes. Scoop out and drain with the zucchini. Set aside.

Put the couscous in a medium bowl. Heat the chicken broth to a boil, pour it over the couscous and stir with a fork until well mixed. Cover the bowl with foil and let sit for 5 minutes. Stir again to separate the grains. Add the zucchini, carrot, basil, and olive oil and toss to mix well. Season to taste with salt and pepper and set aside.

In a small pan, heat the red currant jelly over medium heat until smooth, stirring often. Bring to a boil and boil, stirring until the jelly has reduced and thickened, 1 to 2 minutes. Let cool slightly.

Brush the salmon pieces with red currant jelly. Grill the salmon until just opaque through, about 4 minutes per side, or bake on foil-lined baking sheet for about 12 minutes (the salmon need not be turned when baked). Arrange the salmon on individual plates, spoon the couscous alongside and serve.

Any variety of salmon can be used here, though more delicate chum or pink should be baked rather than grilled.

Red Currant Glazed Salmon
with Couscous Salad

Cajun Barbequed Shrimp

Combine butter, garlic, Worcestershire sauce and seasonings in a large skillet over high heat. When butter is melted, add shrimp and cook for 2 minutes, shaking pan back and forth. Add clam juice, cook and shake back and forth for 2 minutes. Add beer and cook 1 more minutes. Remove from heat and serve immediately.

SERVES 2

1 lb	**jumbo shrimp** shell on, uncooked	454 g
3/4 cup	**unsalted butter**	175 mL
1-1/2 tsp	**minced garlic**	7 mL
1 tsp	**Worcestershire sauce**	5 mL
1 tsp	**cayenne pepper**	5 mL
1 tsp	**black pepper**	5 mL
1/2 tsp	**salt**	2 mL
1/2 tsp	**crushed red pepper**	2 mL
1/2 tsp	**thyme leaves**	2 mL
1/2 tsp	**dried rosemary leaves** crushed	2 mL
1/8 tsp	**dried oregano leaves**	0.5 mL
1/2 cup	**clam juice**	125 mL
1/4 cup	**beer** at room temperature	60 mL

Chef Carol's Fish and Chip Batter

YIELD about 2 cups		
1 cup	**flour**	250 mL
3/4 tsp	**salt**	4 mL
4 tsp	**baking powder**	20 mL
1 cup	**water**	250 mL
	more for thinner batter	

Mix until smooth; the thicker the consistency, the heavier the batter. Thin with water. This batter can be used for any raw fish fillets, onion rings, scallops, clams, etc. Dip food to be fried in batter and place it gently into hot, deep fat. Do not crowd the pan. Turn when golden brown. When brown on both sides, the fish will be cooked.

Curry Sauce for Shrimp

YIELD about 1/4 cup		
2 tbsp	**butter**	30 mL
1/2 tsp	**salt**	2 mL
1 tsp	**curry powder**	5 mL
2 tbsp	**flour**	30 mL
	fresh or frozen shrimp	

Combine all ingredients; add fresh or frozen shrimp. Let simmer for 5 to 8 minutes.

The Greenfield Inn Vodka Cream Seafood Sauce

YIELD 5 cups		
1/4 cup	**butter**	60 mL
1/2 tsp	**red pepper flakes**	2 mL
1/2 cup	**vodka**	125 mL
2 cups	**Italian crushed tomatoes**	500 mL
2/3 cup	**Parmesan cheese** grated	150 mL
1/2 cup	**Romano cheese**	125 mL
1 cup	**whipping cream**	250 mL

Melt butter over high heat until bubbly; add red pepper flakes. Rapidly add vodka and tomatoes and simmer for 2 minutes. (The alcohol burns off, but makes the tomatoes "come alive.") Add the cheeses and simmer for another 2 minutes. Add cream and simmer for 1 minute. Prepare pasta shell or tube pasta according to directions on package; when cooked, mix pasta completely with the sauce and serve over shrimp or any other seafood.

Bread Stuffing for Whole Fish

Melt butter in large skillet over medium-low heat. Add onion and stir until tender, about 5 minutes. Add remaining ingredients and mix well. Use as a stuffing for whole fish.

YIELD 4 3/4 cups

1/2 cup	**butter**	125 mL
1	**medium onion** finely chopped	1
3 cups	**fresh breadcrumbs**	750 mL
1 cup	**cheddar cheese** grated	250 mL
3 tbsp	**fresh parsley**	45 mL
	dash of salt and pepper	

Fort Myers Shrimp Cooking Sauce

Thaw frozen shrimp and peel, leaving the last section of the shell on. Remove sand veins and wash. Preheat frying pan to medium-high. Add oil, salt, pepper and shrimp. Cook for 8 to 10 minutes or until shrimp are pink and tender, stirring frequently. Increase temperature slightly adding vermouth and lemon juice. Cook one minute longer, stirring constantly, and drain. Serve hot or cold.

YIELD 2/.3 cup

2 lbs	**shrimp**	908 g
1/4 cup	**olive oil or salad oil**	60 mL
2 tsp	**salt**	10 mL
1/2 tsp	**white pepper**	2 mL
1/4 cup	**extra dry vermouth**	60 mL
2 tbsp	**lemon juice**	30 mL

Drummond's Ranch Marinade for Fish

Mix all ingredients together and pour over fish. Do not marinate for more than 1 hour, as the fish will begin to cook. Cook fish over charcoal or on a gas grill for 8 to 10 minutes a side.

YIELD 3/4 cup

1/4 cup	**olive oil**	60 mL
1	**garlic clove** chopped	1
1/4 tsp	**cayenne pepper**	1 mL
1 tsp	**grated lemon juice**	5 mL
1	**juice of 1 orange**	1
1 tbsp	**basil** chopped	15 mL
1 tbsp	**parsley** chopped	15 mL
1 tbsp	**soy sauce**	15 mL
1/4 cup	**red onion** chopped	60 mL

Vodka Sauce for Oysters

Pour a dash of vodka and Tabasco over opened oysters. Grill lightly.

Salmon Fillet Hollandaise Sauce

YIELD 3/4 cup

3/4 cup	**butter** plus 1 (5 mL) teaspoon	180 mL
1 tbsp	**white wine vinegar**	15 mL
2 tbsp	**lemon juice**	30 mL
3	**egg yolks**	3
	pinch of salt	

Melt butter in a small saucepan. In a second saucepan bring the wine vinegar and lemon juice to the boil. Blend eggs and seasoning in a blender or food processor. Keeping the motor running, gradually add in the hot lemon juice and wine vinegar. Then gradually add in the hot butter in a steady trickle. The sauce will now thicken. Arrange the sauce on each plate, lay salmon on top.

Parsley Lemon Fish Sauce

YIELD about 1/2 cup

1-1/2 tbsp	**lemon juice**	23 mL
1/4 cup	**butter**	60 mL
1/4 cup	**parsley** chopped fine	60 mL

Melt the butter and add the lemon juice. Stir until blended. Add the parsley.

Mustard Butter Sauce for Fish

YIELD about 1/3 cup

2 tsp	**prepared mustard**	10 mL
6 tbsp	**butter**	90 mL

Melt the butter; add the mustard. Good with lobster.

Lemon Butter Sauce for Fish

Add ingredients to the melted butter and let it foam up but not brown.

YIELD about 1/2 cup

1/2 cup	**melted butter**	125 mL
1	**juice of 1 lemon**	1
1/2 tsp	**lemon rind** grated	2 mL
1/2 tsp	**salt**	2 mL
1/8 tsp	**white pepper**	0.5 mL
1/4 tsp	**grated onion** or 1/2 tsp (2 mL) chopped chives	1 mL

Cucumber Butter for Fish

Melt butter and add the other ingredients except cucumber. Stir in cucumber at the last minute.

YIELD about 1/3 cup

3 tbsp	**butter**	45 mL
1 tsp	**vinegar**	5 mL
1 tbsp	**lemon juice**	15 mL
1/2 tsp	**onion** grated	2 mL
4	**drops hot pepper sauce**	4
1/2 tsp	**salt**	2 mL
	dash white pepper	
3 tbsp	**cucumber** seeded, coarsely grated	45 mL

Newburg Sauce

Melt butter in double boiler; blend in flour and add the cream, stirring constantly, until slightly thickened. Season with salt, pepper and paprika. When about ready to use, beat the egg yolks with a fork and mix with the sherry. Pour a little sauce into this mixture and return all to double boiler. The flour helps prevent curdling; however, the sauce may be made with whipping cream and no flour. Pour over hot shrimp or lobster and stir to blend. Serve at once as standing may curdle the sauce. If not using sherry, add a little more cream.

YIELD 1 1/3 cups

1 tbsp	**butter**	15 mL
1 tbsp	**flour**	15 mL
1 cup	**light cream**	250 mL
1/2 tsp	**salt**	2 mL
	dash of pepper	
	dash of paprika	
3	**egg yolks**	3
1/4 cup	**sherry**	60 mL

Tartar Sauce

Mix all of the ingredients together. Traditionally served with any kind of fish.

YIELD 1 1/3 cups

1 cup	**mayonnaise**	250 mL
4	**small sweet pickles** chopped	4
1 tbsp	**minced onion**	15 mL
2 tbsp	**minced green pepper**	30 mL
2 tbsp	**lemon juice**	30 mL

New Orleans Cocktail Sauce

Mix the ingredients together in the order listed. Stir well and allow to stand to blend flavors. Especially recommended for shrimp cocktail.

YIELD 1 3/4 cups

1/2 cup	**olive oil**	125 mL
2 tbsp	**paprika**	30 mL
1/4 cup	**prepared horseradish mustard**	60 mL
2 tbsp	**parsley** chopped	30 mL
1/4 cup	**white wine vinegar**	60 mL
6 tbsp	**onion** minced	90 mL
2 tbsp	**celery** chopped	30 mL
1/2 tsp	**salt**	2 mL
1/8 tsp	**white pepper**	0.5 mL

Seafood Cocktail Sauce Caribbean

Mix the mayonnaise with sour cream and watercress. Season with lemon juice, anchovy paste, tarragon, hot pepper sauce and garlic. Stir until sauce is smooth and seasonings are blended. Pour sauce over a variety of fresh or frozen seafood, such as lobster, crab, shrimp, clams.

YIELD about 1 3/4 cups

1 cup	**mayonaise**	250 mL
1/2 cup	**sour cream**	125 mL
1/4 cup	**water cress**	60 mL
1 tbsp	**lemon juice**	15 mL
1 tsp	**anchovy paste**	5 mL
1/4 tsp	**tarragon**	1 mL
1/8 tsp	**hot pepper sauce**	0.5 mL
1	**small garlic clove** crushed	1

Smoking fish

Any fish can be smoked, but species high in fat (oil) such as salmon and trout are recommended because they absorb smoke faster and have better texture than lean fish, which tend to be dry and tough after smoking.

Use seasoned non-resinous woods: hickory, oak, apple, maple, birch, beech or alder. Avoid pine, fir, spruce, etc. or green woods. If heavier smoke flavor is desired, add moist sawdust to the heat source throughout the smoking process.

Control heat by adjusting airflow.

Control temperature
Hot-smoking: 90°F for the first 2 hours; 150°F for remaining smoking time.

Cold-smoking: 80–90°F for 1–5 days or more.

Lox: 70–80°F for 1–3 days.

Tips on grilling seafood

1 A hinged wire grill basket is best for cooking whole fish such as salmon. It also works well for fillets of tender fish such as perch, snapper, catfish or flounder.

2 Firm fish, such as salmon, can be cooked directly on the grill if handled carefully.

3 Grill fillets over medium to medium-low heat. Fish can cook quickly and it is easier to slow down cook time and monitor to not over cook.

4 Turn fish only once. (Flipping back and forth will break fish apart.)

5 If using a marinade, allow fish to soak up flavor for at least 30 minutes. Refrigerate while soaking in marinade.

6 If you are going to use the marinade as an extra sauce on top of the cooked fish, the marinade liquid must be boiled by itself for at least 5 minutes to cook out any bacteria that may be there from when the fish was soaking.

Diamond pattern on grilled fish

1 Prior to starting the grill. Pour a small amount of vegetable oil on a paper towel and lightly coat the grill rack. This will help from having the fish stick to your rack. (If the grill's already started, it's usually too hot to get your hand close enough to do it, plus not too safe with the oil.

2 Preheat the grill to medium-high.

3 Brush or pat both sides of the fish lightly with olive oil.

4 Cook without turning on first side for 2 to 3 minutes.

5 Rotate fish 45-degrees on the grill (a one-quarter turn). Cook for 2 to 3 minutes longer.

6 Flip fish to other side and finish cooking time.

Additional cooking time in the microwave

If you're not sure grilled fish is done, you can cook it in the microwave oven for another minute or two. (This can over cook your fish very quickly and make the fish dry or rubbery textured, so watch the timing).

1 Cook fish for half the required time on a barbecue grill. This gives the fish the attractive grill marks and some grilled flavor.

2 Transfer the fish to a microwave-safe baking dish and cook 1 to 2 minutes to finish cooking the fish. Press or flake with a fork to test for doneness.

3 Remember, fish continues to cook after it is removed from the microwave oven so allow 1 to 2 minutes standing time before you cook it any longer.

How to freeze fish

1 Rinse under cold, running water until water runs clear. Pat dry with paper towels. Wrap tightly in plastic wrap, squeezing out all the air.

2 Wrap again in aluminum foil.

3 Write contents and date on a freezer label or strip of making tape.

4 Freeze as quickly as possible.

5 For best results, thaw and use within two weeks.

Credits

It is not without help and encouragement that one is able to even begin the publication of a book. I would like to recognize all of those very special people that have supported me on the Seafood Cookbook. *These people have been dedicated to providing me with the best of the best recipes and photography. I deeply appreciate their help and understanding with this project.*

Photo Credits

Simply Seafood Inc.
1111 North West 45 th Street
Suite B, Seattle, WA 98107
United States

Sandy Krogh, Culinary
Consultant *for her ongoing
support for the wish list.*

Credits

Newfoundland Fisheries
and Aquaculture
Newfoundland & Labrador

California Seafood Council
Santa Barbara, California,
United States

Adelphia Seafood
Reading, PA

Irish Sea Fisheries Board -(BIM)
P.O. Box 12
Crofton Road, Dun Laoghaire
Co. Dublin
Ireland

Florida Seafood Council
United States

Rabbit Hill Inn
Lower Waterford, Vermont

The Inn on the Common
Craftsbury Common, Vermont

Maude's Courtyard B&B
Kennebunkport, Maine

Kalani Oceanside Retreat
Kehena Beach, Hawaii

Dockside Guest Quarters
York, Maine

Rock Eddy Bluff Farm
Dixon, Missouri

The Nautilus House Of
Cape Cod
East Sandwich, MA

Gunflint Lodge
Grand Marais, Minnesota

Brierley Hill
Lexington, Virginia

Quietwood B&B
Sparwood, British Columbia

The Gaslight Inn
Gettysburg, Pennsylvania

Green Springs
St. Francisville, Louisiana

B&W Courtyards
New Orleans, Louisiana

The Bernerhof Inn
Bed & Breakfast

A Taste of the Mountains
Cooking School
Glen, New Hampshire

Whispering Pines
Bed & Breakfast
Dellroy, Atwood Lake, Ohio

The Seal beach Inn and
Gardens Bed & Breakfast
Seal Beach, California

Angel of the Sea
Bed & Breakfast
Cape May, New Jersey

Bethel Point Bed & Breakfast
Harpswell, Maine

Inn on the Sound
Falmouth, Massachusetts

Le Guignol on
Kalakaua Avenue
Chef Shane Sutton

Pilgrim's Inn Bed & Breakfast
Deer Isle, Maine

The Greenfield Inn
Greenfield, New Hampshire

A. Drummond's Ranch
Cheyenne, Laramie, Wyoming

Chef Paul Milne
St. Michaels, Maryland

The 1661 Inn & Hotel
Manisses
Black Island, Rhode Island

The Lodge on Little
St. Simons Island
Chef Charles Bostick, Georgia

Fairview Inn
Fairview, Jackson, Mississippi
Chef Todd McClellan

Three Chimney's Inn
Durham, New Hampshire

Cottage on the Cove
Coupeville (Whidbey Island),
Washington

The Lilac Inn
Brandon, Vermont

The Historic Strater Hotel
Durango, Colorado

York Harbor Inn
York Harbor, Maine

Camano Island Inn
Camano Island, Washington

The Cypress Inn
Conway, South Carolina

Chef Minnie Giraldi
Nina Rossini, Sous Chef

Index

Index

Index